THE ENGINES
OF THE
BROKEN WORLD

Discourses on
Tacitus and Lucan

ALSO BY IAN DALLAS:

Plays:
A Masque of Summer
The Face of Love
Statue of David
Oedipus and Dionysus

Novels:
The Book of Strangers
The Ten Symphonies of Gorka König

Political Theory:
The Time of the Bedouin
Political Renewal
The Interim is Mine

Other Works:
The New Wagnerian

* * *

Collected Works

THE ENGINES
OF THE
BROKEN WORLD

Discourses on
Tacitus and Lucan

IAN DALLAS

First edition: Budgate Press 2012
All rights reserved
budgate@gmail.com

Budgate Press
Postnet Suite 402
Constantia 7848
Cape Town
Republic of South Africa

Subject: Roman history – Roman politics – Classics – Civil war – Critique of bankers

ISBN: 978-0-620-53250-1
Printed by Lightning Source

for Zulaikha

CONTENTS

'Sic, cum conpage soluta
Saecula tot mundi suprema coegerit hora,
Antiquum repetens iterum chaos, omnia mixtis
Sidera sideribus concurrent ignea pontum
Astra petent, tellus extendere littora nolet
Excutietque fretum, fratri contraria Phoebe
Ibit et obliquum bigas agitare per orbem
Indignata diem poscet sibi, totaque discors
Machina divolsi turbabit foedera mundi.
In se magna ruunt.'

(Bellum Civile:
Lucan: I. 72-81)

'So when this world's compounded union breaks,
Time ends, and to old Chaos all things turn,
Confused stars shall meet, celestial fire
Fleet on the floods, the earth shoulder the sea,
Affording it no shore, and Phoebe's wain
Chase Phoebus and enraged affect his place,
And strive to shine by day, and full of strife
Dissolve the engines of the broken world.
All great things crush themselves.'

(Translated by
Christopher Marlowe)

A
MACHIAVELLIAN
PREFACE

Since the idea of using a classical text to illuminate the contemporary crisis derives from Machiavelli's decision to write using the History of Rome by Titus Livy, it seemed he was a fitting point of departure.

He did so because he observed that 'in constituting republics, in maintaining states, in governing kingdoms, in forming an army or conducting a war, in dealing with subjects, in extending the empire, one finds neither prince nor republic who repairs to antiquity for examples.'

Beginning with Rome's origin he observes that all cities are built 'either by natives of the place in which they are built or by people from elsewhere.' The second case occurs when people 'are driven by pestilence or famine or war to abandon the land of their birth and to look for new habitations.'

The twentieth century was marked by two cataclysmic events. Firstly came the mass genocide in Europe of a race, initiated by Germany, and a class, initiated by Russia. Secondly came the mass influx of disinherited masses into Europe. The Turks came to Germany following the dismemberment of the Osmanli Dawlet. The Berbers came from North Africa following the collapse of the French colonial empire. The Indians came from the violent dismemberment of Empire which tore the subcontinent into Pakistan, India and Bangladesh.

As the exhausted people of Europe, utterly betrayed by its political class, watch in fear as the European entity fragments, having been stitched together merely by a common currency without intrinsic value, it becomes daily more clear that renewal can only come from the great mass of displaced people whose binding factor is neither race nor coinage, but religion.

This work should prove relevant to the new Europeans. It may also benefit the great gene-pool of humanity in the '-stans: Uzbekistan, Kyrgyzstan, Tajikistan, Kazakhstan and the Uighurs. If it reaches the Chinese it may be part of the rescue needed to raise them from their present devolved state, for the purport of this work is to tell them that if they live under a system which like ours has separated terminology and definition from natural reality, their fate is collective madness.

The intention of this work, however, is not to rouse the masses, and certainly not to incite insurrection. As the political class stand helpless while their oligarchic masters panic, it is scarcely a time to call for change. It was one of the slogans of that same political class. Our task is to point out that the building has collapsed and then avoid falling masonry.

Machiavelli chose to comment on Livy and he has been taken by the current hegemony to be a champion of the republic. His text 'The Prince' still causes embarrassment not for its realpolitik but for its unbounded admiration for the great Cesare Borgia. He knew his Tacitus, but his pay-masters were in need of re-assurance. Wisely, he admonished them.

> 'There is, in fact, a golden saying voiced by Cornelius Tacitus, who says that men have to respect the past but to submit to the present, and while they should be desirous of having good princes, should put up with them of whatever sort they may turn out to be. And unquestionably those who act otherwise usually bring disaster both upon themselves and upon their country.'

Machiavelli saw leadership as being founded on a correct reading of 'the time' – actions would be determined by that. He broke up time into recognisable units as a doctor measures a fever in units.

Prevedere discosto –
    see from afar and in advance
Conoscere e mali quando nascono –
    recognise the sickness at its birth
Conoscere discosto –
    recognise from afar

La qualità de' tempi –
  the quality of the time: if it is –
        Quieti – tranquil
        Pacifici – peaceful
        Dubbiosi – uncertain
        Avversi – contrary

These conditions, according to him, left one poised between 'fortune' and 'occasion' – the first being the givens of event in which you find yourself and the second that point at which the un-conditioned can break in forming a new conditional reality.

While Cesare Borgia, despite the civil-service dedication to Lorenzo, is the archetypal hero of 'The Prince', yet he is also the flaw in the Machiavellian thesis. At the very moment of triumph – he failed. What he should have done, he did not do. Machiavelli saw this, so can we today. Borgia should simply have killed Pope Julius before his election. He saw it as an error – a wrong choice.

'Errò adunque el Duca in questa electione,
  E fu cagione dell'ultima ruina sua.'

(De Principatibus VII. 49)

'So the Duke's choice was a mistaken one,
and it was the cause of his ultimate ruin.'

This failure to grasp the profound and tragic event
of Borgia's not acting should not, in turn, be seen as
another tactical error. Rather, it was Machiavelli's
not being in the process, not having experience of
the involvement and taste of power play which left
him only with the politique of choices. He resem-
bled Eliot's 'Prufrock' who said:

'No! I am not Prince Hamlet, nor was
    meant to be:
Am an attendant Lord, one that will do
To swell a progress, start a scene or two,
Advise the prince; no doubt, an easy tool,
Deferential, glad to be of use,
Politic, cautious, and meticulous;
Full of high sentence, but a bit obtuse;
At times, indeed, almost ridiculous –
Almost, at times, the Fool.'

This touches on why he chose Livy, who had a
dream of a lost republican vision, so that he could
offer it up as rescue to Lorenzo's republic, already
enmeshed in banking, which would end, torn from

the political encasement, mortgaged to the world bankers of our time.

The great master of politics, Sir Ronald Syme, O.M. explained to us in his 'Tacitus':

> 'Tacitus wrote history with the accent upon personality, penetrating to the deepest recesses in his search for motive. So did Sallust. Fatalism or pessimism is no bar. Sallust puts the individual at the centre of affairs – '

(Tacitus Vol. 2 p. 526)

Tacitus was an insider, an aristocrat and a senator. He married in AD 77 the daughter of Britain's governor, Iulius Agricola. Holding the preatorship he was elected into the Fifteen Colleges, the major religious institute of Rome. His last years were climaxed by being appointed consulate governor of the senatorial province of Asia, and by his writing the Annals. As a historian he never forgot that he was 'in the weave' of Empire. There was no empyrian view. He saw all too clearly how it had happened. There is no doubt, and it is not my intention to prove what Syme's masterworks have already demonstrated, no doubt but that Tacitus had penetrated, decoded, deconstructed, or at least seen – the deception, that primal deception on which the Empire of power was based. He was the archetypal insider, collegiate of state religion, senator and proconsul. He was also remote on the edge of Empire, a Roman in Asia. He is the man who got away.

Lucan is the man who did not get away. One of our greatest poets, and for that reason, certainly one of our most profound historians.

As Ibsen, the master of the human predicament in its self-entrapment, will be required to glimpse the true condition of the financial oligarchs, so it is necessary to turn to Lucan, the master of the nihil of power politics, to glimpse what is implied in our present civic psychosis.

With notable exceptions (Bartsch, Morford, Johnson and Sklenář), classicists seem to stumble when they reach Lucan, not through a failure to come to grips with Lucan's electric style but rather through a common failure to understand the weltanschauung of the world they live in, itself one of the themes of the poet. One writer notes: 'His 'Libertas' is not our democratic freedom.' This assumes that there is something called democratic freedom, and one we agree to call ours. It assumes that the two terms are co-habitable in our age, when one is not free to mint coin or print one's own currency, let alone open one's own bank. It assumes that the masses do choose their own governance.

The classicists, with noble exceptions, imagine that they live in a world where they can teach Tacitus and Lucan. Machiavelli insisted that it was Tacitus and Lucan who could teach us. M. Annaeus Lucanus (AD 39-65) was the son of M. Annaeus Mela. Born into a wealthy family, he was also the nephew of Seneca. Born in Cordoba, he was brought as a child to Rome. In AD 60 at a festival in honour of the Emperor, Lucan praised Nero in his poem and was promptly given a state position. Then, after defeating Nero in a poetry contest he was forbidden by the demented Emperor to write or recite. The mental and moral disintegration of Nero was swift and dramatic, the tyrant rapidly indulging his terror of conspiracy in ordering forced suicides. By AD 65 Lucan was composing the tenth book of his epic when he became involved in the plot to assassinate the Emperor, plotted by Piso. He was arrested in the hysteria of the royal response to the conspiracy and condemned to state-ordered suicide. His uncle, Seneca, in a cruelly extended suicide, due to his aged body's capacity for survival, calmly accepted his end.

To examine Lucan's 'Bellum Civile' is to uncover what Jane Arden called 'the Other Side of the Underneath'.

I

In his introduction to 'The Roman Revolution' Syme states:

> 'In all ages, whatever the form and name of government, be it monarchy, republic, or democracy, an oligarchy lurks behind the facade; and Roman history, Republican or Imperial, is the history of the governing class.'

It must be remembered that two events found it useful to raise the understanding of the Roman

Republic from what it had been to a model which stood for government of the people by the people.

The French and American Revolutions consciously offered themselves as realisation of the lost Republican model. In the post-Revolutionary vocabulary Republic was good, that is, just, and Empire was bad, that is, tyranny. This was an invention, a propaganda.

> 'When the patricians expelled the kings from Rome, they were careful to retain the kingly power, vested in a pair of annual magistrates; and though compelled in time to admit the plebeians to political equality, certain of the great patrician houses, Valerii, Fabii and Cornelli, none the less held in turn a dynastic and almost regal position.'

He goes on to explain:

> 'The consulate did not merely confer power upon its holder and dignity for life; it ennobled a family forever. ... It was a scandal if a man without ancestors aspired to the highest magistracy of the Roman Republic.'

'Consulatum nobilitas inter se per manus tradebat.'

(Sallust: Bellum Iugurthinum LXIII.6)

'The nobles passed the consulate from hand to hand within their own order.'

Syme's definition is this:

'As an oligarchy is not a figment of political theory, a specious fraud, or a mere term of abuse, but very precisely a collection of individuals, its shape and character, so far from fading away on close scrutiny, at once stands out, solid and manifest. In any age of the history of Republican Rome about twenty or thirty men, drawn from a dozen dominant families, hold a monopoly of office and power.'

Nevertheless, what was preserved in the Republic was an arena in which senators and proconsuls could work out the affairs of state. Debate and free speech were not trivialised as they are today in an age that has a whole technology devoted to their dissemination, yet has a pre-ordained set of what may not be said. This Republican freedom was not just speech but an existential embodying in individuals of the point of decision making. Cicero was forced to suicide in order to silence him. Cato chose suicide as a refusal to endure a world which would forbid him his speech, that was, to him, his programme.

Mommsen dates the end of the Republic neither with Caesar's crossing of the Rubicon, although it presaged all that followed, nor with Actium and the triumph of Octavianus. He insists that it occurred on the occasion of the battle of Thapsus on the 16th of April 46 BC. This battle effectively ended the Caesar/Pompeius civil war. It was, and surely this was Mommsen's point, what led to Cato's suicide. At Utica, Cato said to his son, 'I grew up in freedom, with the right to free speech. I cannot change my ways in my latter years and accustom myself to slavery. But it is right that you, having been born and brought up under these conditions, should serve the divinity that governs your destiny.' On the news of his death at Utica, Caesar said, as if standing over the corpse, 'I envy you this death, for you envied me the chance to save you.' Here Caesar was arrogantly imposing his pardon on a corpse that he could never pardon alive. In almost exact replica of that moment we find Napoleon regretting the execution of the Duc d'Enghien whose crime also had been to be the living embodiment of what he opposed. The event – the victorious processional of Caesar, now unopposed, could proceed within its internal dynamic – could be seen as destiny, but over and against it stood the existential protest of Cato, its ineradicable negation.

'Victrix causa diis placuit, sed victa catoni.'

(Lucan)

'The victorious cause pleased the gods, but the defeated cause pleased Cato.'

From Sulla, through the Cataline conspiracy to the Civil War the Republic's fabric was disintegrating. Caesar knew its days were numbered. He declared, 'The res publica is nothing – a mere name without body or shape.' Even as early as 54 BC Cicero had said, 'It has lost not only all its sap, all its blood, but even its colour and its earlier shape.' In 'De re publica' he even admitted: 'In times of emergency only a dictator could help,' yet adding, 'but later should take his place among the principes.'

The Republic, while it had never been the ideal model of equality as in modern readings, had by its balance and its limited dimensions been a state which gave its citizens a voice in open debate through a values-based senatorial elite. The Republic was also war, and war meant expansion. The statal model of consultation and rhetoric slowly buckled under the emergence of the gigantism of Empire. Sulla's intervention heralded the caesarism to come.

'Sulla quoque inmensis accessit cladibus ultor. Ille quod exiguum restabat sanguinis urbi hausit; dumque nimis iam putria membra recidit, excessit medicina modum, nimiumque secuta est, qua morbi duxere, manus.'

(Lucan: Bellum Civile II. 139-143)

'And then, to crown the infinite slaughter, came Sulla's vengeance. What little blood was left at Rome he shed; and while he lopped off too fiercely the limbs that were corrupt, his surgery went beyond all bounds, and his knife followed too far on the path whither disease invited it.'

It is of the Sullan imposition on Republican modes that Tacitus utters a judgment that the centuries have not failed to reconfirm.

'Et corruptissima re publica plurimae leges.'

(Annals III. 27)

'And laws were most numerous when the commonwealth was most corrupt.'

Sulla's crisis intervention brought with it a whole set of laws, inhibitions and prohibitions. What Tacitus tells us is that this event of protective legislation came with a double aspect. The one proclaimed aspect was to react vigorously to the threat to the Republic. The laws dealt with the new situation. Crisis management. The other aspect was that precisely these laws swept away those fundamental givens on which Roman freedom was founded.

Again it is the legal sanctioning of the rescuer which marks a further disintegration of what had yet still called itself Republic.

'Tum Cn. Pompeius, tertium consul corrigendis moribus delectus et gravior remediis

quam delicta erant suarumque legum auc-
tor idem ac subversor, quae armis tuebatur
armis amisit.'

(Annals III. 28)

'Cneius Pompeius was then for the third
time elected consul to reform public morals, but in applying remedies more terrible
than the evils and repealing the legislation
of which he had himself been the author,
he lost by arms what by arms he had been
maintaining.'

Tacitus' 'quae armis tuebatur armis amisit' must
stand not only as the definition of the American
President who ordered the Iraqi invasion, but also,
alas, as the epitaph of humanist Europe.

After Pompeius came the challenge from Julius
Caesar. The Republic was set on its path to self-
destruction when one man made his fateful choice
to rebel. The crossing of the Rubicon, thus entering
the frontier of Rome with the 13th Legion, meant
both defiance and dominance. Suetonius wrote
that on crossing the river he declared, 'Iacta alea
est.' The die is cast. Lucan, always at the heart of

things, wrote that he said, 'Temerata iura relinquo.'
Here I leave the law, dishonoured as it is. From
that decision came the ultimate defeat of Pompeius
and Caesar's own assassination. There followed
the defeat of the Republican murderers, Brutus
and Cassius, and the creation of Octavianus as
the new Caesar in Triumvirate, established by the
Proscriptions, that is, expropriation and slaughter.
With three reduced to one, came the monarchic
transfer from Republic to Empire. Octavianus
became Augustus Caesar.

Tacitus:

> 'Exim continua per viginti annos discor-
> dia, non mos, non ius; deterrima quaeque
> impune ac multa honesta exitio fuere.'

> 'There followed twenty years of continuous
> strife, custom or law there was none; the
> vilest deeds went unpunished, while many
> noble acts brought ruin.'

In the end, 'in his sixth consulate Augustus annulled
the decrees of his Triumvirate – '

> 'Sexto demum consulatu Caesar Augustus,

potentiae securus, quae triumviratu iusserat
abolevit deditque iura quis pace et principe
uteremur.'

(Annals III. 28)

'and gave us a constitution which might
serve us in peace under a monarchy.'

Tacitus speaks in open contempt of the new dispensation, able to do so under the Trajanic inter-
lude of sound government.

'Acriora ex eo vincla, inditi custodes et lege
Papia Poppaea praemiis inducti ut, si a
privilegiis parentum cessaretur, velut parens
omnium populus vacantia teneret. sed altius
penetrabnat urbemque et Italiam et quod
usquam civium corripuerant, multorumque
excisi status.'

'Henceforth our chains became more gall-
ing, and spies were set over us, stimulated
by rewards under the Papia Poppaea law, so
that if men shrank from the privileges of
fatherhood, the State, as universal parent,
might possess their ownerless properties.

But this espionage became too searching,
and Rome and Italy and Roman citizens
everywhere fell into its clutches.'

Something had happened. It was not the events.
It was not even the individual actors on the scene.
It was not immorality. An inner dislocation of the
experiencing self had – over the long time-span
from Sulla to Augustus (from the primal dictator
to the absolute dictator) – taken place that was
deeper than the acts of enslavement. The Roman
citizen, son of the Republic, had been enslaved, but
it was not the gladiator's enslavement. Spartacus
could rebel, but the citizen could not. This was a
quite new achievement, the forging of an obedient
slave, to all accounts free, enjoying the circus and
the spectacle. Here, our contemporary species was
born.

By the time of Domitian, who came after the com-
plete outer structure of Empire had collapsed in
the year of the three Emperors, this new slavery
had been established as the new reality.

Pliny told Domitian:

'Iubes esse liberos: erimus.'

You bid us be free – and we will be free.'

A devolutionary process had been set in motion and once it had achieved its rational political deconstruction it had also by that token arrived at a quite different kind of men. Tacitus in the Histories goes into a detailed analysis of the disintegration of Empire and the irrevocable loss of even the Augustan deception which resulted in a condition that was to continue in flux but always the same until the whole affair collapsed, a metaphysical fantasy replacing the ruined metaphysical pseudo-reality of Rome as Empire. The Roman Empire vanished and the Holy Roman Empire emerged. The German slave states had become the masters and the religion of the persecuted minority had elevated their man into god, metaphysic as the replacement of the failed cycle that had degenerated from emperor into god to being merely ordinary man into emperor.

Tacitus once he had confronted the primal deception, at its beginning so linear and understandable and at its end so intricate and incomprehensible, knew that to unlock what the pattern hid from men could only be revealed if he went back to the beginning. If he lived in an age where the vast structure made men, he had to go back to that point where men had made the structures – how, and why. He had arrived at the who of it.

Thus, from the History emerges the Annals.

The History deals with the total breakdown of the Empire. AD 69. The year of the three Emperors. Yet that is not just the breakdown of the dynastic Augustan Empire. It exposed the primal deception on which Augustus had built his tyranny of tranquillity. In Syme's definition:

'The Principate arose from usurpation.'

(P. ix Vol. I Tacitus)

That Augustan event is in turn based on the struggles between an increasingly weakened republican order and a series of increasingly powerful dictators, singly or in triumvirate power. That phase prior to the Augustan deception called principate is therefore in itself a process of the self-destruction of a societal model due to the rising dominance of powerful individuals. From Sulla, through a series of conspiracies, power passed not by senatorial debate but by civil war to Pompeius, then Caesar, then Antonius and finally to Augustus.

All that followed the Tacitean era of Trajan and then Hadrian presaged a long future of Empire but already pre-designed and to a degree pre-determined by the political mode that had emerged as a result of these primal traumata.

Speaking of the crisis that followed the assassination of Nero leading to the disaster of Galba, Otho and Vitellius, Tacitus said:

'Evolgato imperii arcano, posse principem alibi quam Romae fieri.'

(History I. 4)

'For now had been divulged that secret of the Empire, that Emperors could be made elsewhere than at Rome.'

Professor Haynes brilliantly exposes in her Commentary on the Histories, 'The History of Make-Believe', underlying the secret of Empire confronting the collapse of the dynastic doctrine Tacitus was unveiling the primal imperii arcano:

the erection of the Empire was founded on the obliteration of the Republic.

It implied that Empire could continue as long as you had some kind, any kind, of an Emperor. As to the record of the debacle following the opening of the dynastic to a leadership in effect chosen by the army, the Legion, Tacitus turned to the 'Annals' to penetrate more deeply into the very psychology of personal governance, no more asking how did it happen but who made it happen, even to asking 'What happened?'

Syme had said that 'narrative is the essence of history', Tacitus set about telling the story of the State from Tiberius through to Nero.

In my lifetime the emerging oligarchy of financiers started right from the beginning of their reign at Bretton Woods. They laid down a necessary ideological position to protect their hidden position in modern society. History, their scriptwriters decreed, was not, could not be narrative. Events were too complex. People did not make history, history made history. Flux did it! Sociology measured the present – social structures, modified and remodelled. There was even a whole class of people to, in turn, be seen not as individuals but as mere heads of groups, political parties. A political system was framed to sustain unhindered the rapacious take-over of the world's resources by the new oligarchs. To prevent revolution the two-party government was established, thus sustaining a continuum of conflict inside the system. History, then, had to be seen as the sociology of the past.

The 'Wars of the Roses' were re-assessed as a conflict caused by what one pseudo-historian had defined as 'bastard-feudalism', other historians, assured of a Chair, rushed to debate and expand interpretation of ancient events through a term invented only a semester before. The logic of historical theory ended up with the conclusion that in fact the Wars of the Roses had never taken place.

At the same time Alison Weir's densely researched history of the same epoch which laid bare precisely the who and why of the Wars was dismissed as a mere novel. Weir's predecessor, C. V. Wedgwood, an important and eloquent historian, had already been condemned to oblivion. So out went Gibbon, Schiller, Mommsen, Froude, Carlyle, in short the ongoing discourse of the Tacitean attempt to lay bare what and who caused events to happen.

I

Half a century later the narrative tradition emerged, enfeebled, to recount the day a certain event had happened, or even the hours that preceded a catastrophe. We now could know the grisly details of Marie Antoinette's last humiliating tumbril ride through the streets of Paris and every step she took up to the guillotine, but how she got there and who else was involved apart from the executioner was reduced to the background noise of social tectonics grinding and splitting.

In one of the great passages of the History, Tacitus lays bare the stage on which his tragic story will unfold and be examined, as he prepares in Syme's definition to confront 'the ineffable complexities of authentic history.' (Roman Revolution: ch. 4)

> 'Trepidam urbem ac simul atrocitatem recentis sceleris, simul veteres Othonis mores paventem novus insuper de Vitellio nuntius exterruit, ante caedem Galbae suppressus ut tantum superioris Germaniae exercitum descivisse crederetur. tum duos omnium mortalium impudicitia ignavia luxuria deterrimos velut ad perdendum imperium fataliter electos non senatus modo et eques, quis aliqua pars et cura rei publicae,

sed vulgus quoque palam maerere. nec iam
recentia saevae pacis exempla sed repetita
bellorum civilium memoria captam totiens
suis exercitibus urbem, vastitatem Italiae,
direptiones   provinciarum,   Pharsaliam
Philippos et Perusiam ac Mutinam, nota
publicarum cladium nomina, loquebantur.
prope eversum orbem etiam cum de prin-
cipatu inter bonos certaretur, sed mansisse
G. Iulio, mansisse Caesare Augusto victore
imperium; mansuram fuisse sub Pompeio
Brutoque rem publicam: nunc pro Othone
an pro Vitellio in templa ituros? utrasque
impias preces, utraque detestanda vota inter
duos, quorum bello solum id scires, deteri-
orem fore qui vicisset. erant qui Vespasianum
et arma Orientis augurarentur, et ut potior
utroque Vespasianus, ita bellum aliud
atque alias cladis horrebant. et ambigua de
Vespasiano fama, solusque omnium ante se
principum in melius mutatus est.'

(History I. 50)

'The alarm of the capital, which trembled
to see the atrocity of these recent crimes,
and to think of the old character of Otho,

was heightened into terror by the fresh news about Vitellius, news which had been suppressed before the murder of Galba, in order to make it appear that only the army of Upper Germany had revolted. That two men, who for shamelessness, indolence, and profligacy, were the most worthless of mortals, had been selected, it would seem, by some fatality to ruin the Empire, became the open complaint, not only of the Senate and the Knights, who had some stake and interest in the country, but even of the common people. It was no longer to the late horrors of a dreadful peace, but to the recollections of the civil wars, that men recurred, speaking of how the capital had been taken by Roman armies, how Italy had been wasted and the provinces spoiled, of Pharsalia, Philippi, Perusia, and Mutina, and all the familiar names of great public disasters. "The world," they said, "was well-nigh turned upside down when the struggle for empire was between worthy competitors, yet the Empire continued to exist after the victories of Caius Julius and Caesar Augustus; the Republic would have continued to exist under Pompey and Brutus.

And is it for Otho or for Vitellius that we are now to repair to the temples? Prayers for either would be impious, vows for either a blasphemy, when from their conflict you can only learn that the conqueror must be the worse of the two." Some were speculating on Vespasian and the armies of the East. Vespasian was indeed preferable to either, yet they shuddered at the idea of another war, of other massacres. Even about Vespasian there were doubtful rumours, and he, unlike any of his predecessors, was changed for the better by power.'

Professor Haynes, herself tuning into the Tacitean deconstruction or rather unmasking of the power template, lays bare the dynamic of the crisis of Empire.

'Tacitus shows us that by the time of the Histories the symbolic fiction has become the fiction of a fiction: the people no longer invent emperors as gods; they invent nobodies as emperors.'

(The History of Make-Believe: Haynes: p. 14)

The unfolding of this ultimate nihilism in which not only is nothing (the oligarchy) and nobody (the Emperor) what it presents itself as, also requires that people (the Empire) believe that the charade and the actors are genuine, while also aware that all is false. Accepting the pretences (oligarchy, Empire, Emperor) as the real world demands a dislocation between nature and event which implies that survival depends on transforming a psychosis into a reality. Thus the fully evolved post-Claudian Empire makes men complicit in a madness which demands total collaboration from the Legion, the magistrates, the Senate, the Emperors themselves, and the citizens.

Tacitus openly shows himself as one living inside the dream-reality.

'Ulteriora mirari, praesentia sequi; bonos imperatores voto expetere, qualiscumque tolerare.'

(History IV. 8)

'I may regard with admiration an earlier period, but I can acquiesce in the present, and, while I pray for good Emperors, I can endure whomsoever we may have.'

He also lifts the veil to expose natural (i.e. non-statal) reality lurking there ready to shatter the agreed on madness.

Clemens, a former slave of Agrippa Postumus, on the death of his master passed himself off as the deceased Agrippa. The man was arrested and brought before Tiberius.

> 'Percontanti Tiberio quo modo Agrippa factus esset respondisse fertur "quo modo tu Caesar."'

> (Annals II. 40)

> 'When Tiberius asked him how he had become Agrippa, he is said to have replied, "As you became Caesar."'

In order to grasp this descent from functioning government among men to the psychosis that Empire became, the stages of transformation must be identified.

There are three stages. The first happens with enormous speed over roughly only two generations. The second is the long period of tyranny and peace. The third begins with the collapse of dynastic rule, the Julio-Claudians, and abruptly crashes with the year of the three assassinated claimant Emperors.

Phase One

The consultative frame of the Republic buckled under the triumphs that saw the destruction of Carthage, the annexation of both Spain and Greece. Failure to reform led to the Italian peoples rising against Roman authority. The military class, the Legion, which had once been the affair of local farmers, had become the recruiting instrument of landless men without loyalty. These soldiers became pawns in the power struggle of the Republic's elite. Rome became a zone of mob violence. Sulla emerged as the rescuing dictator. His reign of terror involved a mass execution of senators and the leading families of Rome. Once in power he tried to reform the Senate to reflect the now enormous territory of the State. He raised the Senate from 300 to 600, the Quaestors to 20 and the Praetors to 8. Tribunal legislation had to be ratified by the Senate. He returned power to the new civil administration and then retired from public life. Rome, the Republic, however, now stood indefensible before the political possibility of another military take-over from within.

Gnaeus Pompeius emerged as the dominant military defender of the Republic. After triumphs from Spain to Asia Minor he returned to enter Rome in 62 BC to celebrate his third Triumph.

Insecure against envy and resentment from the Senate, Pompeius took Crassus and Caesar as his allies to form the Triumvirate that indicated the historical end of republican rule. When Crassus was killed by the Parthians it left the two great Generals centre stage. The Senate in their crisis attempt to rescue the political structure appointed Pompeius as sole Consul in 52 BC.

Caesar was then faced with his historic decision. He marched in 49 BC and the result was civil war. Forced by the Senate Pompeius engaged Caesar, and although outnumbered, Caesar defeated him at Pharsalus and Thapsus. On the news of Caesar's victory Cato committed suicide rather than lose his freedom to dictatorship. By 47 BC Caesar was absolute master of Rome. In 44 BC he announced that he was dictator for the restoration of the commonwealth. Dressed in royal robes he refused the title. The model of a republican dictator had been designed. On the 15th of March 44 BC, he was assassinated.

Caesar's end was the end of that first stage, but it had, as it were, an interval before the curtain rose on the second act. It involved the convulsions required to transform Octavianus into Augustus Caesar.

The confrontation had to happen in order to end the phase of Caesar's assassination. This played out as pitting the defenders of the Republic, that is Caesar's assassins, Brutus and Cassius, against the Caesar faction in quest of punishment. It was nothing less than the death of the Republic faced with the death of Caesar. Octavianus the inheriting nephew and Antonius the loyal ally met up with the Republican defenders at Philippi. With the loss of Cassius, the strategist, Brutus was doomed. Antonius removed his purple cloak and draped it over the body of Brutus, his former friend, according to Plutarch. In Syme's magisterial phrasing:

'This time the decision was final and irrevocable, the last struggle of the Free State. Henceforth nothing but a contest of despots over the corpse of liberty. The men who fought at Philippi fought for a principle, a tradition and a class – narrow, imperfect and outworn, but for all that the soul and spirit of Rome.'

(Syme: Roman Revolution p. 205)

Again a triumviral dictatorship was in command, Octavianus, Antonius and Lepidus. As before it swiftly became a duel between Octavianus and Antonius, the lover of his mother, Servilia. The task facing the young Octavianus was double, to defeat Antonius and his Republican cause, then transform his enemy into the enemy of Rome and claim the cause of the Republic as his matter.

The struggle was for monarchy, and the outcome would be monarchy. Antonius in settling for an Eastern dominion gave Octavius exactly the scenario he needed to redesign his enemy as a decadent orientalist and traitor to the cause of Rome.

Phase Two

The defeat of Antonius and Cleopatra at the Battle of Actium opened the way to the era of Augustus. Politics was over, now there would only be permitted the passive record of events, art and literature. No more great men, only great monuments and epic poems.

On the 13th of January 27 BC, Octavianus formally surrendered his power to the Senate.

On the 16th of January 27 BC the Senate bestowed on Octavianus the title of Augustus as head of the New Order, 'res publica restituta'.

This was the profound dislocation at the foundations of the Roman State, a monarchy, a dynastic monarchy now declared itself a reborn republic. It called itself a Principate. The name no longer mattered.

According to Mommsen: 'The Principate had three fathers: Caesar, Augustus and Tiberius.' (A History of Rome Under the Emperors, p. 81). Caesar initiated the system when he wore the kingly robes but refused the title. Augustus set up the system by construction of a new oligarchy and an embedded Senate. Tiberius opened the way to an absolute monarchism that saw the sovereignty of the people obliterated.

The judiciary became obsolete. From AD 19 onwards no more laws were passed by the assembly but by the Senatus consultum, which as Mommsen observed, 'effectively eliminated the Roman people as a component in the law-making process.'

Tiberius' first governmental act was to have magistrates elected in the Senatorial curia and the results then announced on the Campus Martius.

Within this Mommsonian survey of the Augustan power transfer should be set his observation that: 'He is not above the law: the law is above him.'

While that was the brilliant modus operandi of Augustus, so that various rights remained with the Senatorial system, nevertheless, imperial provisos opened the way to the later, piece by piece, assimilation of Senatorial authority.

Everything that was to follow lay under the condition of the Legion of the new regime. The standing army was a legal institution. Its officers were appointed by the Emperor. Here, Mommsen said, was the core of power. 'The sword ruled.'

Mommsen wrote his assessment under the Second Reich. Awarded the Nobel Prize just before his death in 1902, he could not have imagined that in the shortest time, following the cataclysm of a World War, a Republican elected system would succumb to a dictatorship which in 1938 would take to itself command of the Wehrmacht, an action which in turn would lead that army to total obliteration on the fields of Russia.

In the Augustan system as established by Tiberius the military imperium was a magistracy yet the imperator was never elected by the people, but proclaimed by the soldiers.

Under the bankers' hegemony it must not be forgotten, narrative history had to be abolished and was replaced by useless structural models, not, apparently, the work of individual men. Mommsen, Germany's intellectual giant, had to be dragged from his plinth. Scrutiny of the Roman Republic risked exposing the new imperial model of financial power as being not Republican but totalitarian.

Mommsen, according to Prince von Bülow, was a ferocious opponent of Bismarck. He wrote his masterwork on the brink of a new society which would first transform democracy into dictatorship and then after an apocalyptic war re-baptise mass slavery as democracy and create a kind of ur-Augustan principate in which the actual princeps would be hidden from view and unknown by name to the masses. Despite all the social re-designing nothing had changed but the names. Just as Rome remained an oligarchic society from Romulus to Constantine, so too did Germany from the 1938 Chancellor up until today. A venerable German who had been an aide to Field Marshal von Hindenburg told me that from that time up to the present day, 'The same people sat at the high table of the German State.'

If one were to draft an introduction to a book returning history to the modern university one could propose a summary of Roman history thus:

'The Republic: nobodies running something.
The Civil Wars: somebodies running nothing.
The Empire: nobodies running everything.'

To give Mommsen the last word on Empire:

'What, above all, made the Principate so nefarious was its utter dreariness, emptiness and poverty of spirit. The Emperors ushered in total intellectual senility.'

To give Augustus the last word on the Emperor there is Suetonius' narrative:

'He asked for a mirror and ordered that his hair be combed and his weakened jaw propped up. When his friends had been admitted, he asked whether he seemed to them to have played the comedy of life well, and he added this verse (in Greek); "Since the play has gone well, give your applause / and send us all away with your thanks."'

(Div. Aug. 99.1)

Coinage.

The Emperor minted coin in massive quantities, the Senate modestly. The Emperor minted gold and silver. Copper was assigned to the Senate. Minting was not a source of income. Minting coin is the root of power.

It follows that wherever the currency is controlled remains the seat of power. Whoever – unmasks the Imperial throne.

Phase Three

The third stage of the Roman State is the one which involves a total collapse of all the new foundational principles of the Empire as defined by Augustus and Tiberius. Augustus left a dynastic monarchy run by an obedient civil-service Senate, and empowered by an Emperor controlled Legion. Right from the start the dynastic principle began to unravel. The chosen grandsons of his daughter Julia and his faithful Agrippa both died. Augustus appointed his wife's son by her first marriage, Tiberius. He, in turn adopted Germanicus, the last link with the Julian blood-line. Thus, in Tiberius, the Julio-Claudian dynasty was secure. His rule was submitted to devastating analysis in Tacitus' 'Annals' – one which must be examined after the debacle of AD 69 when the whole edifice fell apart. The Histories tell the story of 'what' and it was the inadequacy of the structuralist explanation which drove Tacitus to examine the epoch of

Tiberius and bring into the historical discourse the great 'who' which places the individuals again at the centre of the destined events.

With Germanicus assassinated the dynastic snake curled round first Caligula, then Claudius, then Nero. Each, in turn, assassinated and with the Julio-Claudian dynasty at an end, Rome was back in Civil War. Only this time there were no great issues of freedom and tyranny, no complex leaders ambitiously reaching for power, no voice of reason. The year 69 AD was the year of the three Emperors – they were the Civil War – but it was also the year when the Emperors became extras in the struggle. There were no heroes opposing them. This was an action movie. The Legions were the stars.

II

Tacitus begins his 'History' with the bleakest of overviews.

'Opus adgredior opimum casibus, atrox proeliis, discors seditionibus, ipsa etiam pace saevum. quattuor principes ferro interempti: trina bella civilia, plura externa ac plerumque permixta: prosperae in Oriente, adversae in Occidente res: turbatum Illyricum, Galliae nutantes, perdomita Britannia et statim omissa: coortae in nos Sarmatarum ac Sueborum gentes, nobilitatus cladibus

mutuis Dacus, mota prope etiam Parthorum
arma falsi Neronis ludibrio. iam vero Italia
novis cladibus vel post longam saeculorum
seriem repetitis adflicta. haustae aut obrutae
urbes, fecundissima Campaniae ora; et urbs
incendiis vastata, consumptis antiquissimis
delubris, ipso Capitolio civium manibus
incenso. pollutae caerimoniae, magna adul-
teria: plenum exiliis mare, infecti caedibus
scopuli. atrocius in urbe saevitum: nobilitas,
opes, omissi gestique honores pro crimine et
ob virtutes certissimum exitium. nec minus
praemia delatorum invisa quam scelera, cum
alii sacerdotia et consulatus ut spolia adepti,
procurationes alii et interiorem potentiam,
agerent verterent cuncta odio et terrore. cor-
rupti in dominos servi, in patronos liberti; et
quibus deerat inimicus per amicos oppressi.'

(History I.2)

'I am entering on the history of a period
rich in disasters, frightful in its wars, torn
by civil strife, and even in peace full of horrors. Four emperors perished by the sword.
There were three civil wars; there were more
with foreign enemies; there were often wars

that had both characters at once. There was success in the East, and disaster in the West. There were disturbances in Illyricum; Gaul wavered in its allegiance; Britain was thoroughly subdued and immediately abandoned; the tribes of the Suevi and the Sarmatae rose in concert against us; the Dacians had the glory of inflicting as well as suffering defeat; the armies of Parthia were all but set in motion by the cheat of a counterfeit Nero. Now too Italy was prostrated by disasters either entirely novel, or that recurred only after a long succession of ages; cities in Campania's richest plains were swallowed up and overwhelmed; Rome was wasted by conflagrations, its oldest temples consumed, and the Capitol itself fired by the hands of citizens. Sacred rites were profaned; there was profligacy in the highest ranks; the sea was crowded with exiles, and its rocks polluted with bloody deeds. In the capital there were yet worse horrors. Nobility, wealth, the refusal or the acceptance of office, were grounds for accusation, and virtue ensured destruction. The rewards of the informers were no less odious than their crimes; for while some seized on consulships and priestly offices, as their share of the spoil, others on procuratorships, and posts of more confidential authority, they robbed and ruined in every direction amid universal hatred and terror. Slaves were bribed to turn against their masters, and freedmen to betray their patrons; and those who had not an enemy were destroyed by friends.'

The deception to which the modern reader studying Tacitus, and indeed the other great Latin scholars, may succumb is that they should transpose the terminology of Rome over to the present day without first reading the modern situation free of its simplistic annexation of the Roman political vocabulary.

Just as Augustus is not the same as Mithridates, Perseus or Hannibal, by the same reading the Roman Emperors are not Hitler or Stalin.

Galba, the first of the three post-Nero Emperors, informs Piso:

'Neque enim hic, ut gentibus quae regnantur, certa dominorum domus et ceteri servi, sed imperaturus es hominibus qui nec totam servitutem pati possunt nec totam libertatem.'

(History I.16)

'It is not here, as it is among nations despotically ruled, that there is a distinct governing family, while all the rest are slaves. You have to reign over men who cannot bear either absolute slavery or absolute freedom.'

Here the claimant Emperor is defining what had been the Augustan model at its inception, poised stylishly between Republic and Empire – the undefined Principate maintaining the Senate but reducing them to servants of an Imperial and hereditary Constitution. Yet, already, post-Nero, Rome is in an Empire-state deprived of its sacral hereditary foundation, the Julio-Claudian line.

It is this descent by layers from Republic to Emperor-with-Senate, to absolutist Emperor with civil-service-Senate which ends up with an Emperor, without inheritance, claiming the acclamation of the Legion as the new legitimacy.

This descent into a military-based absolutist model which will become the final mode of Empire can be recognised in the modern models of Europe and America all based on the Roman template with Germanic additions.

Modern Britain gives us a similar layered descent into the totalitarian model, that is to say not the superficial intervals of European dictatorship.

Stage One – A King with a controlling Parliament – i.e. Senate. The Senate (Parliament, remember) starts to rise in power over the Magistrate class. Its leader redefines himself not in the House, but in signing a treaty, as Prime Minister, a title never confirmed in the Statute Books. In order to give him that leadership his Conservative Party had to have Queen Victoria raise him to the Peerage. In order to do this he was required to purchase a country house and land making him one of the gentry.

As Lord Beaconsfield, Benjamin Disraeli, Prime Minister, proposes the nation build the Suez Canal offering a swift access to Indian waters. The House (Senate!) debate the amount of the project. Disraeli retires to a private room where Rothschild, the banker, patiently waits. Rothschild accepts the government's proposed fee. Disraeli returns to the House with its bid accepted. Power has passed from the Senate to the Oligarchs.

Stage Two – Disraeli proposes that the Queen declare herself, via Parliament, Empress of India. In one move, two results.
One: Empire is created – while named a political democracy.
Two: The private East India Company is discreetly absorbed into the political framework of the government 'India Office'.

Stage Three – Private enterprise under a brilliant oligarch, Cecil Rhodes, sets up gold and diamond mining in South Africa. Expanding further, Rhodes transforms a territory into a new country he names Rhodesia (following Alexander's practice). Challenged by resident Dutch settlers he triggers a war which forces British intervention.

Stage Four – A peace treaty establishes the Union of South Africa as a political entity tied to the Crown. The new country's finance remains within a fiduciary system of world banking, supporting a civil service and technical elite, leaving the masses uneducated, unhoused and unfed.

Empire, as term, remains within the Principate modus operandi of a passive civil-service Parliament (Senate) and a military loyal to the Crown. Power has passed to another group in society – at the same time that that group takes power it enforces an anti-elitist, anti-hereditary social doctrine. 'Why should they inherit vast wealth and governance just by the ACCIDENT of birth?' As this doctrine is applied, death-duties, inheritance tax and titles devalued – the new oligarchy absorbs these principles to itself.

By the twenty-first century a ruling hereditary oligarchy is in place on a near-global scale using a fully global system of interlocked fiduciary instruments and institutions.

The Augustan model of peace at home and war on the periphery collapses as the Roman masses – that is American and European peoples – begin to turn against the now brutally taxing parliaments and senates (the Senate in the model), forcing the need to set police and military on the rebel masses. That is, of course, civil war itself. The father in the police fires on the demonstrating son.

III

The disappearance of power in the outlines of state and society and its apparent replacement with token symbolic structures, iconic leadership and a necessary vocabulary to render the whole theatre of governance seem real, that is, ideology, marked the devolutionary unravelling we have examined from Sulla to the Three Emperors.

In the same manner this classical deconstruction of state power can be recognised once it has been granted that the contemporary stage is not what it pretends. Once the modern political discourse is set aside on the acknowledgement of modern capitalism as psychosis rather than system based on logic, and once the self-explanatory (ideological) version of today's crisis is set aside, it becomes possible to identify in the modern narrative a disturbing relevance and indeed similarity to the classical contortions of the primal state crises of ancient Rome.

In America in its first post-civil-war phase it is possible to confirm the existence of an elite ruling group bonded together in a republican mode. It is an age dominated by sophisticated and ambitious oligarchs disporting themselves in a political arena that claims to be the model of the new democracy.

Men like Theodore Roosevelt, Henry Cabot Lodge and Henry Adams were closely bonded by being part of the tiny ruling elite, by being Protestant, and by the conviction that men governed their own affairs. The original inhabitants were now subdued, slaughtered or shut away in Reservations. The powerful new wealth of the Lodge-Adams generation allowed them to look out beyond the frontiers of their now peaceful Republic.

Tacitus had given warning:

'Sed vobis maximum discrimen, penes quos aurum et opes, praecipuae bellorum causae.'

(History IV. 74)

'Yours is the greatest danger for you have gold and wealth, and these are the chief incentives to war.'

Brooks Adams, the brother of Henry, wrote to Roosevelt:

'The one hope for us, the one chance to escape from our slavery, even for a year, is war, war which shall bring down the British Empire.'

(M. Josephson:
The President Makers)

Already the vision of Empire crystallised itself in the admission that their ascension required the descent of the present world Empire on which the sun never set, Britain's. The next generation of Roosevelts would dedicatedly commit themselves to Britain's demise, and succeed brilliantly.

However, just as externally an emergent America implied an end to British hegemony, so too, internally, the exclusivist Protestant elite would soon be challenged by 'new money' from another religiously bonded group, the New York jews. Henry Adams called the Republicans 'The Bankers' Party' (Letters of Henry Adams, vols 4-6).

Theodore Roosevelt wrote of attending "a huge lunch by the Seligmans, where at least half of the guests were Jew bankers; I felt as if I was personally realising all of Brooks Adams' gloomiest anticipations of our gold-ridden, capitalist-bestridden, usurer-mastered future." (Letters of Theodore Roosevelt, vol. 1)

The ghastly record of the 20th century has left a double legacy which has obscured the most important developments of our age. On the one hand has been the ferocious savagery of the anti-jewish doctrines using race as the key integer of their ideology, which ended in the mass murder of European jews by the million in the Nazi years. On the other hand the post-Holocaust period in the second half of the century led to a total abstention from identifying the banking elite as being jewish. Once the racist doctrine was condemned that link, too, had to be forbidden. Let us set aside, intellectually unacceptable as it is, the race ideology.

Firstly, and it is the most potent factor against the jew-as-capitalism ideology, it cannot be forgotten that the majority of the revolutionary Politburo of Lenin was jewish. This indicates that among jewish intellectuals its leadership was marxist and anti-capitalist. In mid-century almost all the leading jewish intellectuals in America were communist or supporters of the Left, at the time used as a racist accusation of treachery to the U.S., but an important proof today of their abhorrence of capitalism.

Clearly, in turn of the century America, the jewish community was driven by the ruthless exclusivity of the Protestant christian elite, to bond themselves together not just as businessmen but as social beings. The end result of this situation was twofold. It empowered its members to survive using the methods of their excluding and despising masters. The method was internal family inheritance and inter-marriage between group members. As the Almanach de Gotha mapped out the power system after Napoleon, while the political class still ruled actively ("Senate" in our model), so a parallel Almanach was forged, marriage by marriage, merger by merger, within the emerging banker class.

America from 1898 began its unstoppable march to Empire. From Puerto Rico, to Cuba on to the Philippines, it was clear that what had been a political entity governed by a mutually consultative elite – that is, a Republic, had mutated into a dynamic instrument of expansion and conquest. America, to achieve this, had to resort to that identical ruse forced on Augustus when he transformed the State into a structuralist machine which had no more place for open debate, in other words, no more place for a moral measure that could be imposed on the imperial programme.

This permits us to recognise that with the Adamses, the Roosevelts, Reed and Lodge, America had a kind of Julio-Claudian line that made Empire seem to be Republic. The 'Pledge of Allegiance' was written in 1892. Victory and World War II saw the end of the Roosevelt line, and the brief leadership of Eisenhower, hero of war, ended patrician rule. On his departure from office he made his famous warning that 'democracy', the Principate of the Roman model, was now endangered by the 'military-industrial complex', it being the enemy of a state still governed by an elite under benign orders.

The three Presidents bundled together in a crisis of legitimacy, Nixon, Ford and Carter, represent a pattern of change quite similar to the disaster of the three assassinated Emperors of Rome which led to a fateful metamorphosis of governance, an Empire which had utterly abrogated those principles and values for which Brutus, Cato and even Cicero had lived and died.

That the State had changed utterly was made clear by the election of a Hollywood film actor to the Presidency. Under Ronald Reagan the dismantling of Senatorial power was masked by the open transformation of wealth inside the economic frame of society itself.

'Dum histrio cubiculum principis insultaverit, dedecus quidem inlatum, sed excidium procul afuisse.'

(Annals XI. 28)

'"When an actor," they said, "impudently thrust himself into the imperial chamber, it certainly brought scandal on the State, but we were a long way from ruin."'

Reagan did not bring ruin. On the face of it he brought renewal and an expanded market. However, what his arrival did bring was a recognition by intelligent people that something fundamental had changed in the political framework of power. It was not that the State should not be governed by an actor, but rather, that this indicated something more profound. It meant that power had passed from the political class (the Senate) to another grouping. There was, there had been, there was occurring, an oligarchic shift. Eisenhower, the great military strategist, had seen it coming. From Reagan to second Bush the changes inside the USA were scarcely affected by outside events. Inside the country there was a transformation. During that time the banking fraternity moved from passive guardians of capital to an active fiduciary colonisation of private wealth. Just as the tank and the bomber transformed warfare from battle to obliteration, so the leveraged buyout, the merger and the acquisition turned finance into a control mechanism.

Unfortunately, the bankers' hidden power situation also meant that they had acquired along with a servile Senate the old order's ambitions of Empire.

Roosevelt, flushed with the success of the Cuban annexation, wrote:

> 'It is a great historical expedition, and I thrill to feel that I am part of it. If we fail, of course we share the fate of all who fail, but if we are allowed to succeed (for we certainly shall succeed, if allowed) we have scored the first great triumph in what will be a world movement.'

(Letters of Theodore Roosevelt, vol. 2)

President McKinley followed the band. He wrote: 'We need Hawaii just as much and a good deal more than we did California.' ('In the Days of McKinley': Leech) That was on May 4. On June 15, Hawaii was annexed. The Senate – in our Roman model – the House of Representatives (Congress) passed confirmation by 209 to 91. It was this scenario which was to surface just as the new oligarchy had seized the reigns of power in the last decade of the 20th century.

The internal transformation of the American society played itself out against a ferocious battle by the ruling Protestant christians as they stubbornly kept the jewish financiers from access to, let alone control of finance. J. P. Morgan, Morgan Grenfell, Kidder Peabody closed ranks in the crises of the thirties to exclude a jewish presence. This hatred was not uniform. The Harrimans and the Rockefellers linked and joined the great jewish families. Paul Cabot of Boston took the Goldman Sachs patriarch to lunch at his club. Brook took Cabot aside and said: "You know perfectly well that jews are not allowed in the dining room." Cabot resigned on the spot. Three decades later, learning that his Omaha club refused jews, Warren Buffet, future partner of Goldman Sachs, did the same and then joined a country club of the jewish community.

When Admiral Darlan, former Vichy minister of Petain, turned up at the wartime White House and held out his hand to Weinberg, the latter placed his visiting-card in it and said: "There my boy, go find me a taxi!" Furious at Roosevelt's indifference to Nazi persecution, after the war, Weinberg crossed over to Eisenhower's Republican administration. This helped him secure Treasury and Defence for his men. He crossed back to the Democrats for Kennedy and Johnson. Politics had become passive. Finance, or as it now called itself, the Market, had become active.

The anti-jewish campaign came to an end in the 70s when the head of Goldman Sachs, Gus Levy, became the first jewish president of the New York Stock Exchange Council of Governors. Once dominant, in power they preferred inclusivity. Goldman Sachs were to be found in Israel and the Arab Emirates. Their chief, Lloyd Blankfein, was the creator of "Islamic" banking! Another dialectic had imposed itself, making the old theatricality of anti-jewism irrelevant. It was best defined by one of the founding causes of the old enmity, Benjamin Disraeli, who wrote:

> 'Two nations between which there is neither connection nor sympathy, and which are not even governed by the same laws. These two nations are the rich and the poor.'

As the previous elite, watched over by the political class, fell to ruin in over-exposure to the masses, understandably the emerging elite, led by the financial class, rose to power in remaining hidden to the masses. Secrecy they renamed confidentiality. They could even publically boast their practice of secrecy as a moral virtue. The French Lazard family of bankers openly declared their motto: "The secret of the Lazards is their secret." In directories across the world, opposite the great bankers' names could be found the legend: Profession – Philanthropist. Art galleries were founded, museums funded and charities flourished. Wittily, a psychosis was defined as conspiracy theory, thus shunting off into the asylum anyone who had identified the genuine conspiracy practice that was capitalism.

It took two thousand years before the details of the oligarchy that was the social reality of the Augustan Empire were revealed in Ronald Syme's 'Roman Revolution', a work which at one instant not only changed classical studies but challenged the whole foundation of the modern State.

IV

The rise of the new oligarchy created by America's bid for Empire, which we can date from 1898, followed slavishly to the course of decline that was to be expected.

As the deception of the Republican claim floundered before America's surge over Europe in the Thirty Years' War (as defined by Ernst Nolte, the German historian) 1914-1945, the age of political giants ceded to the democratic dwarfs. First, a President accused of corruption has to resign to avoid impeachment, next, a President is impeached for lying about a sexual peccadillo. The low level of political leadership year by year indicated that the masses were slowly realising that the ones in charge were not, by necessity, the ones in charge.

Obedient to the new oligarchic power the politicians obediently propagated the financiers' doctrines as social health. The politicians themselves raised the cry to 'get government off our backs'. The call to get government out of the market, on the face of it an old-fashioned free-trade slogan, now meant that government's role was to strip itself of its own powers.

In Britain the Conservative Party chose a woman as their leader. She was the daughter of a shopkeeper and first emerged as the housewife politician. She was promptly whisked off to Zurich where, isolated and under guard, she was indoctrinated by Europe's leading monetarists into the language and necessary policies to re-tune Britain as a money-market centre, thus obliging her on taking office to dismantle the country's former industrial base. As Prime Minister, Margaret Thatcher proved an obedient and forceful servant of finance. Front bench debate gave way to Select Committees held in camera, and that in turn transformed premiership into virtual dictatorship.

'Versa ex eo civitas et cuncta feminae oboed-
iebant, non per lasciviam, ut Messalina,
rebus Romanis inludenti. adductum et
quasi virile servitium: palam severitas ac
saepius superbia; nihil domi impudicum,
nisi dominationi expediret.'

(Annals XII. 7)

'Then came a revolution in the State, and
everything was under the control of a
woman, who did not, like Messalina, insult
Rome by loose manners. It was a stringent,
and, so to say, masculine despotism, there
was sternness and generally arrogance
in public, no sort of immodesty at home,
unless it conduced to power.'

By the time the American based oligarchy was
ready to invade Iraq, the psychotic British Prime
Minister was able to steer the nation into a bloody
war without benefit, unopposed, despite opposition from Cabinet, Parliament and people.

The spectacle of the Socialist Party's Cabinet,
despite all its pacifist and populist declarations,
utterly succumbing to a staring-eyed, hypnotised

Premier, and plunging the nation into a pointless American war, left the country in the doldrums of a numb despair.

Tacitus:

> 'Minus triginta transfugae et desertores, quos centurionem aut tribunum sibi eligentis nemo ferret, imperium adsignabunt?'

> (History I. 30)

> 'Shall less than thirty runaways and deserters whom no one would allow to choose a tribune or centurion for themselves, assign the Empire at their pleasure?'

The war itself was initiated by a mere handful of men. One of its key figures was not even elected to government, and, after the conflict was established, was appointed head of the World Bank. Another, in charge of Defence, when confronted with the exposure of an American prison in Iraq holding filmed spectacles of torture and sexual degradation which shocked the rest of the world, simply said, "Things happen!"

Tacitus:

'Suscepere duo manipulares imperium populi Romani transferendum et transtulerunt.'

(History I. 25)

'Thus two common soldiers undertook to
hand over control of the Roman Empire –
and succeeded.'

The apparent power system of Empire in the Julio-
Claudian mode was in reality the dictatorship that
followed the collapse of the illegitimate inheritors,
that is, in the mode of the Three Emperors. So it
was that following the Nixon-Ford-Carter debacle the American Empire soon unravelled into
the phase of dictatorship. It was the dictatorship
that made possible the invasion of Iraq and then
Afghanistan. The necessary legislation stripping
the State of all its Republican traditions of justice,
right of trial and refusal of retention without trial
or cause, was rushed with mass approval through
the Senate. The obedience of government implied
the passive indifference of the people.

'Postquam vero nationes in familiis habemus, quibus diversi ritus, externa sacra aut nulla sunt, conluviem istam non nisi metu coercueris. at quidam insontes peribunt. nam et ex fuso exercitu cum decimus quisque fusti feritur, etiam strenui sortiuntur. habet aliquid ex iniquo omne magnum exemplum quod contra singulos utilitate publica rependitur.'

(Annals XIV. 44)

'But now that we have in our households nations with different customs to our own, with a foreign worship or none at all, it is only by terror you can hold in such a motley rabble. But, it will be said, the innocent will perish. Well, even in a beaten army when every tenth man is felled by the club, the lot falls also on the brave. There is some injustice in every great precedent, which, though injurious to individuals, has its compensation in the public advantage.'

The political scientist, W. D. Burnham, named the mass of citizens who saw no reason to vote, 'the largest political party in America.' One of the few great writers in America after Faulkner, Joan Didion, identified the modern, transmuted entity of governance as:

> '...that small but highly visible group of people who, day by day and through administration after administration, relay Washington to the world, tell its story, agree among themselves upon and then disseminate its narrative. They report the stories. They write the op-ed pieces. They appear on the talk shows. They consult, they advise, they swap jobs, they travel with unmarked passports between the public and the private, the West Wing and the Green Room. They make up the nation's permanent professional political class.'

Pinpointing with deadly accuracy the evidence of the demise of the masses' role in the power she quotes a Republican strategist challenging the Washington Post in September 1998: 'Who cares what every adult thinks? It's totally not germane to this election.' Didion defines the nature of rule as a process and its personnel as: 'A self-created and self-referring class, a new kind of managerial elite... that handful of insiders who invent, year in and year out, the narrative of public life.'

Didion's definition of American democracy clearly is a demonstration that the word has been stripped of even assumed modern meaning. America has become nothing other than a state in a post-Augustan dictatorship posing as the original Republic. The decade that followed Didion's critique precipitated America into the ruin of its inner structure following the disastrous project of its usurper leaders forcing on the nation its unwanted and final bid to maintain Empire status, the invasions of Iraq and Afghanistan. The protective measures of Security, the agonised but acquiescent position on torture and rendition, none of the structural defence of the State could avoid the erosion of the morale of society itself.

The internal tissue of the body politic, what Montesquieu had called 'the Spirit of the Laws', had begun to decay. A generation were brought up on television fantasies which told them that the country had been invaded by two alien races, the vampires and the werewolves. The blood-sucking vampires clearly were the job-stealing Mexicans, and the ancient race of werewolves were the tenacious indigenous 'Indian' population hiding in their reservations. Soldiers openly torturing and killing combatants and urinating on the corpses of the enemy clearly were a far cry from the heroic G.I.'s of World War II.

In his 'Bellum Catalinæ', Sallust explains:

'Sed ubi labore atque iustitia res publica crevit, reges magni bello domiti, nationes ferae et populi ingentes vi subacti, Carthago aemula imperi Romani ab stirpe interiit, cuncta maria terraeque patebant, saevire fortuna ac miscere omnia coepit. Qui labores, pericula, dubias atque asperas res facile toleraverant, eis otium, divitiae, optanda alias, oneri miseriaeque fuere. Igitur primo pecuniae, deinde imperi cupido crevit: ea quasi materies omnium malorum fuere. Namque avaritia fidem, probitatem ceterasque artis bonas subvortit; pro his superbiam, crudelitatem, deos neglegere, omnia venalia habere edocuit. Ambitio multos mortalis falsos fieri subegit, aliud clausum in pectore aliud in lingua promptum habere, amicitias inimicitiasque non ex re sed ex commodo aestumare magisque voltum quam ingenium bonum habere. Haec primo paulatim crescere, interdum vindicari; post, ubi contagio quasi pestilentia invasit, civitas immutata, imperium ex iustissumo atque optumo crudele intolerandumque factum.'

(Sallust. B. C. X)

'But when our country had grown great through toil and the practice of justice, when great kings had been vanquished in war, savage tribes and mighty peoples subdued by force of arms, when Carthage, the rival of Rome's sway, had perished root and branch, and all seas and lands were open, then Fortune began to grow cruel and to bring confusion into all our affairs. Those who had found it easy to bear hardship and dangers, anxiety and adversity, found leisure and wealth, desirable under other circumstances, a burden and a curse. Hence the lust for power first, then for money, grew upon them; these were, I may say, the root of all evils. For avarice destroyed honour, integrity, and all other noble qualities; taught in their place insolence, cruelty, to neglect the gods, to set a price on everything. Ambition drove many men to become false; to have one thought locked in the breast, another ready on the tongue; to value friendships and enmities not on their merits but by the standard of self-interest, and to show a good front rather than a good heart. At first these vices grew slowly, from time to time they were punished; finally, when the disease had spread like a deadly plague, the state was changed and a government second to none in equity and excellence became cruel and intolerable.'

What this means is that the realm of events must not obscure from us the realm of lived experience. Events are themselves that erosive chemical that transforms a raw material into a molecularly different alloy.

'Nolite existumare maiores nostros armis rem publicam ex parva magnam fecisse. Si ita res esset, multo pulcherrumam eam nos haberemus: quippe sociorum atque civium, praeterea armorum atque equorum maior copia nobis quam illis est. Sed alia fuere, quae illos magnos fecere, quae nobis nulla sunt: domi industria, foris iustum imperium, animus in consulundo liber neque delicto neque lubidini obnoxius. Pro his nos habemus luxuriam atque avaritiam, publice egestatem, privatim opulentiam. Laudamus divitias, sequimur inertiam. Inter bonos et malos discrimen nullum, omnia virtutis praemia ambitio possidet. Neque mirum; ubi vos separatim sibi quisque consilium capitis, ubi domi voluptatibus, hic pecuniae aut gratiae servitis, eo fit ut impetus fiat in vacuam rem publicam.'

(Sallust B. C. LII. 19-23)

'Do not suppose that it was by arms that our forefathers raised our country from obscurity to greatness. If that were so, we should have a much fairer state than theirs, since we have a greater number of citizens and allies than they possessed, to say nothing of arms and horses. But there were other qualities which made them great, which we do not possess at all: efficiency at home, a just rule abroad, in counsel an independent spirit free from guilt or passion. In place of these we have extravagance and greed, public poverty and private opulence. We extol wealth and foster idleness. We make no distinction between good men and bad, and ambition appropriates all the prizes of merit. And no wonder! When each of you schemes for his own private interests, when you are slaves to pleasure in your homes and to money or influence here, the natural result is an attack upon the defenceless republic.'

In our time we have participated, and watched passively as a great period of time has come to an end, as it now, in effect, has. What now is recognisable, as the walls crumble and the buildings go up in flames, as the outraged masses riot in protest at the great deception, is that it is over. A world that stretched, metamorphosis after metamorphosis, over centuries, has finally come to an end.

As the great thinkers of the last century, Heidegger, Schmitt and Jünger, all insisted: the time had come, after the nihil, for a new nomos on the earth.

Malaparte, Italy's greatest modern writer, indicated that with the end of World War II, also came the end of a whole epoch.

'Eravamo uomini vivi in un mondo morto.

Non avevo più vergogna d'essere un uomo. Che m'importava che gli uomini fossero innocenti o colpevoli? Non v'erano che uomini vivi e uomini morti, sulla terra. Tutto il resto non contava. Tutto il resto non era che paura, disperazione, pentimento, odio, rancore, perdono, speranza. Eravamo sulla vetta di un vulcano spento. Il fuoco che per migliaia d'anni aveva bruciato le vene di quel monte, di quella terra, di tutta la terra, s'era spento a un tratto, e ora poco a poco la terra si raffreddava sotto i nostri piedi. Quella città laggiù, sulla riva di quel mare coperto di una crosta lucente, sotto quel cielo ingombro di nuvole tempestose, era popolata non già d'innocenti e di colpevoli, di vincitori e di vinti, ma d'uomini vivi vaganti in cerca di che sfamarsi, d'uomini morti sepolti sotto le macerie delle case.'

(Malaparte: La Pelle:
p. 1327 Mondadori)

'We were living men in a dead world. I was no longer ashamed of being a man. What did it matter to me whether men were innocent or guilty? The earth contained only living

men and dead men. All the rest counted
for nothing. All the rest was nothing but
fear, despair, repentance, hatred, bitterness,
forgiveness and hope. We were on the sum-
mit of an extinct volcano. The fire which
for thousands of years had burned the veins
of this mountain, of this soil, of the whole
earth, had suddenly been quenched, and
now little by little the ground was cooling
beneath our feet. That city down below us,
standing on the shore of a sea covered with
a shining crust, beneath a sky heavy with
storm clouds, was inhabited not, indeed,
by the innocent and the guilty, the victors
and the vanquished, but by living men who
were roaming about in search of the means
to allay their hunger and dead men who lay
buried beneath the ruins of the houses.'

The present crisis can only be understood if we
can learn to take in the movement in the zone of
events as taking in – not the immediate and new
catastrophe as isolated disaster, the mythic 'breaking news' – but the sweep of decades, themselves
part of centuries. The end certainly was the global
end of war in 1945 at its inception, but over half
a century in which the oligarchy changed hands,

its final end was the failure of that new power system to survive the collapse in turn of its religion in 2008.

V

With the History, Tacitus both surveys and analyses the disintegration of the Roman State. On the Empire that was to emerge after the four assassinated Emperors, Tacitus, in that interim of relative calm, was relatively free at last to speak, well, almost openly about the Imperial system that was to totter on for centuries to come. So, he determined to go back before the catastrophe and examine, not Augustus with his kind-of civic success, his Principate, but rather that stage when it in turn fell into decay, terror and corruption. Augustus had handed his Principate/Empire to Tiberius. He was all that was left if Julio-Claudian D.N.A.

was to be preserved. For a time the Tiberian epoch proved viable. Yet it in turn fell apart and from its ruin came that fatal family inheritance that was Caligula, Claudius and Nero.

Sir Ronald Syme's definition, "Narrative is the essence of history," is clearly his Tacitean position. Events are going to happen. The storm will certainly break. However, who is at the helm and how the crew respond, will determine if the ship founders or sails out into calm seas. Tacitus's great opus was to be the Annals, that is the history of the Augustan project from Tiberius to Nero. The form of the work, covering each year in detail, drove him by the inner logic of his choice, to search for the pivotal dynamics which determined individuals to act.

In the History he had arrived at the stopping-place of the historian, there, where crisis explodes, where event happens.

'Vetus ac iam pridem insita mortalibus potentiae cupido cum imperii magnitudine adolevit erupitque; nam rebus modicis aequalitas facile habebatur. sed ubi subacto orbe et aemulis urbibus regibusve excisis securas opes concupiscere vacuum fuit, prima inter patres plebemque certamina exarsere. modo turbulenti tribuni, modo consules praevalidi, et in urbe ac foro temptamenta civilium bellorum.'

(History II. 38)

'That old passion for power which has been ever innate in man increased and broke out as the Empire grew in greatness. In a state of moderate dimensions equality was easily preserved; but when the world had been subdued, when all rival kings and cities had been destroyed, and men had leisure to covet wealth which they might enjoy in security, the early conflicts between the patricians and the people were kindled into flame. At one time the tribunes were factious, at another the consuls had unconstitutional power; it was in the capital and the forum that we first essayed civil wars.'

He continues:

'Mox e plebe infima C. Marius et nobilium saevissimus L. Sulla victam armis libertatem in dominationem verterunt.'

(History II. 38)

'Then rose C. Marius, sprung from the very dregs of the populace, and L. Sulla, the most ruthless of the patricians, who perverted into absolute dominion the liberty which had yielded to their arms.'

Tacitus had correctly pinpointed the very moment at which the action to destroy the Republic had occurred, and who the protagonists were. The modern structuralists from simple materialists to complex marxists insist that given the disorder of the Republic, if Sulla had not done it someone else would simply have to have obliged. They avoid the very trap of their system. Firstly, it is a hypothesis which is pre-determined to non-action. Secondly, it would have resulted in another future without Pompeius and Caesar, without Pharsalus and without Actium.

If the Sullan dictatorship lay far in the past and had the benefit of wise historians, and if the recent events of the demise of the Julio-Claudian dynasty, from Tiberius to Nero, had no record while they were in power, now Tacitus could speak "without bitterness or partiality". Given this independence he was free to plunge into that deepest zone of what could still claim to lie within history, there, where the inner drives of men burst out into action, there, where men emerge.

Tacitus devoted the first six books of the Annals to the Tiberian epoch. He examined in detail the strange course of the Emperor's life, from lonely exile in Rhodes, to devious but admirable dictator. He examined how that first phase of his rulership was not only worthy yet already insecure. Haunting his authority and security as ruler was the powerful presence, or rather distant absence of Germanicus. Germanicus, embedded in the Julio-Claudian gene-alogy, was also an enormously popular and brilliant commander. Forced to adopt him, Tiberius felt aware that this man loomed over his rule, a menace, and worse, a desirable alternative to the masses. It seems certain that Tiberius had him poisoned, at least Germanicus himself was convinced. With his death a political inhibition was removed.

The next vital actor in the Emperor's reign was the head of the Praetorian Guard, Sejanus. For sixteen years substantive power lay in the ruthless hands of Sejanus while Tiberius was again in exile from Rome, this time on Capri. Restless after the execution of his powerful co-opted ruler he moved from house to house, finally settling in what had been the country-house of Lucullus.

Tacitus in Book Four (AD 23-28) singles out the arrival of Sejanus into the hall of power as the dividing point of Tiberius' rule.

'C. Asinio C. Antistio consulibus nonus Tiberio annus erat compositae rei publicae, florentis domus (nam Germanici mortem inter prospera ducebat), cum repente turbare fortuna coepit, saevire ipse aut saevientibus viris praebere. Initium et causa penes Aelium Seianum cohortibus praetoriis praefectum.'

(Annals IV. 1)

'The year when Caius Asinius and Caius Antistius were consuls saw Tiberius in the ninth year of his reign: the State was in good health, and the Imperial household prosperous, for he considered Germanicus' death as a piece of good fortune, when suddenly fortune began to run amok, and

Tiberius himself to turn to cruelty or lend support to those who practised it. The cause and origin lay with Aelius Sejanus, commander of the Praetorian cohorts.'

At the end of Book Six he gives his obituary assessment of Tiberius's rule which ended with his death at the age of seventy-eight, smothered under the orders of Macro who in turn had dispatched Sejanus and taken over the Praetorian Guard.

'Dein Rhodo regressus vacuos principis penatis duodecim annis, mox rei Romanae arbitrium tribus ferme et viginti obtinuit. morum quoque tempora illi diversa: egregium vita famaque quoad privatus vel in imperiis sub Augusto fuit; occultum ac subdolum fingendis virtutibus donec Germanicus ac Drusus superfuere; idem inter bona malaque mixtus incolumi matre; intestabilis saevitia sed obtectis libidinibus dum Seianum dilexit timuitve: postremo in scelera simul ac dedecora prorupit postquam remoto pudore et metu suo tantum ingenio utebatur.'

(Annals VI. 51)

'On his return from Rhodes he ruled the Emperor's now heirless house for twelve years, and the Roman world, with absolute sway, for about twenty-three. His character too had its distinct periods. It was a bright time in his life and reputation, while under Augustus he was a private citizen or held high offices; a time of reserve and crafty assumption of virtue, as long as Germanicus and Drusus were alive. Again, while his mother lived, he was a compound of good and evil; he was infamous for his cruelty, though he veiled his debaucheries, while he loved or feared Sejanus. Finally, he plunged into every wickedness and disgrace, when fear and shame being cast off, he simply indulged his own inclinations.'

Tacitus is forced to ask the question about the determining factors around political inheritance, a question reaching beyond the issue of dynastic principle.

'An, cum Tiberius post tantam rerum experientiam vi dominationis convulsus et mutatus sit, G. Caesarem vix finita pueritia, ignarum omnium aut pessimis innutritum, meliora capessiturum Macrone duce, qui ut deterior ad opprimendum Seianum delectus plura per scelera rem publicam conflictavisset?'

(Annals VI. 48)

'Was it probable that, when Tiberius with his long experience of affairs was, under the influence of absolute power, wholly perverted and changed, Caius Caesar, who had hardly completed his boyhood, was thoroughly ignorant and bred under the vilest training, would enter on a better course, with Macro for his guide, who having been selected for his superior wickedness, to crush Sejanus had by yet more numerous crimes been the scourge of the State?'

Thus when Tacitus concludes his view of Tiberius' epoch he arrives at a position which reaches way beyond any subjective biographism. He does not terminate with an abstract political theory, as Lord Acton did in reducing Tacitus's phrase to just that. 'Absolute power corrupts absolutely.'

Tacitus had observed and recorded in detail how

the lessening of restraints over phases of the dictator's life, not just through events but through, step by step, the removal of key people around him – the perfect shadow prince, Germanicus, and then that series of dominating Roman matrons, and finally the dazzling and usurping military leader, Sejanus – with their disappearance there was simply nothing left to stop him, or no-one. To appreciate the full sophistication of Tacitean thinking one must take in that he extends this corruptive process not only over the ruler's life, but by extension, indicates an inescapable imprinting on the next Emperor, already pre-programmed to imagine that power can be possessed and wielded.

Montesquieu in his massive attempt to give body to laws and, by implication, constitutions, 'L'espirit des lois', is today seen as pleading a sociology to be imposed on structuralist politics. Referring to the destruction of the Republic he tells us not to blame specific individuals, rather, he insists, 'we must blame Man, whose craving for power grows each time he gains in power, and who, because he has much, comes to want everything.' In one word he backs away from the liberating, existential clarity of Tacitus and plunges back into that ideological frame of ideas which in itself is surely the modernist version of stoicism. It is Man. 'Ti na kanoume?' as the Greeks say: what can we do? Worse. Since the Tacitean reality places action at the door of the actor, what then does that imply about the silent Senate overseeing the Tiberian, and indeed Augustan, reigns of terror? Waves of mass executions – at home or abroad – by extension point not just to a passive government but to an active body of executioners and an impassive, even indifferent citizenry.

On examining the historic process at this Tacitean level what is unveiled? It becomes clear that titles and pronouncements do not necessarily indicate the seat of power. Already, way before the disaster of AD 69 and the murder of four Emperors in one year, there has emerged a transfer of power. It has moved from the Senate to the Emperor, and then, almost immediately it has begun to settle in a new grouping in society. The Legion. From Sejanus to Macro power can be identified moving to the military institution and its elite, and from it will come Emperors and the making of Emperors. From this too can be recognised that it was not paranoia that drove Tiberius to resent and fear Germanicus. Germanicus had powerful Legions under his command and had their loyalty as well.

If the Tacitean model is applied today, from Senate, Emperor, Legion, in flow of force, there should be outlined another set of integers: Parliament. Political Leader. Bankers. That in turn implies that the bankers must be exposed.

VI

It is now time to apply the Syme model to the crisis of 2008.

> 'As an oligarchy is not a figment of political theory, a specious fraud, or a mere term of abuse, but very precisely a collection of individuals, its shape and character, so far from fading away on close scrutiny, at once stands out, solid and manifest.'
>
> (Syme: The Roman Revolution)

In 1913 in 'Our Financial Oligarchy', Louis Brandeis, a Supreme Court Judge, wrote:

'The dominant element in our financial oligarchy is the investment banker.'

From 1947 the new oligarchy began to lay down its mechanisms and dynamics of power. Its swift evolutionary development was due to its own inner ambition and greed, but it also relied on an increasingly complex set of instruments and measurings so that over half a century a body of technical terms and practices were functioning globally across world markets yet understood by only a few thousand. Where up until the early nineteenth century there still were intellectuals who struggled with the doctrines of the Trinity, transubstantiation, papal infallibility, episcopal initiation and Purgatory, now the academic world re-grouped its studies around:

> high-yield debt
> securitization
> arbitrage trading
> derivatives
> credit default swap
> interest rate swap

Academic research was to spin around new financial concepts, structures and theories:

the Black-Scholes model
deregulation doctrines
efficient market hypothesis

While the theories chased the legal re-defining parameters, banking itself surged ahead of its own constantly expanded limits. Legislation was still accommodating the demands of banking while its practices broke the rules in the rush to profit. The first sign of the system failing came with the small players, hitting not the new mega-rich but the recently buoyant money-class. The Savings and Loan Banks began to collapse. Between 1985 and 1992 over 2000 of these banks failed, peaking in 1989 with a loss of 534.

Over the last decade of the twentieth century the political class demonstrated their increasing sub-servience to the burgeoning financial elite. More and more openly it could be observed that the reward to politicians who favoured banking dereg-ulation and extended powers was to be brought into the executive structure of the mega-banks.

- The Riegle-Neal Act 1974 removed restric-tions on inter-state banking.
- The Gramm-Leach-Bliley Act 1999

demolished remaining barriers between commercial and investment banking.
- The Commodity Futures Modernisation Act 2000 prohibited Federal regulation of over-the-counter (O.T.C.) derivatives.

Gramm left the Senate to become a vice-chair at UBS Warburg.

In 2007:
- Jamie Dunn of JPMorgan Chase earned $34 million
- Lloyd Blankfein of Goldman Sachs earned $54 million
- John Tain of Merril Lynch earned $84 million
- John Mack of Morgan Stanley earned $41 million

Also in 2007:

8 February: The first sign of the sub-prime crisis. HSBC declare a loss of $10.5 billion on unpaid mortgages in U.S. market.

2 April: New Century, the U.S.' second largest housing credit company, collapses.

18 July: Bear Stearns announces failure of two of its speculative funds.

31 July: German bank KfW urgently steps in to

	rescue IKB Deutsche Industriebank. The German state injects €3.5 billion in the rescue package.
6 August:	Belgian bank Fortis, Royal Bank of Scotland and Banco Santander take over the Dutch ABN Amro. At €71 billion it is the biggest fusion in financial history.
9 August:	BNP freezes three sub-prime credit funds. The E.C.B. releases €94.8 billion in response.
17 August:	The Fed lowers interest rates from 6.25% to 5.75%, the first of many to come.
22 August:	Europe, Britain and Central America's central banks together release 330 billion liquidity into the system.
23 August:	Bank of America invests $2 billion into Countrywide Financial.
21 October:	Stanley O'Neal, head of Merril Lynch, resigns and announces a loss of $2.24 billion.
4 November:	Charles Prince of Citigroup resigns.

This was the preliminary set of tremors which announced the coming earthquake of 2008.

In 2008:

8 January:	James Cayne of Bear Stearns resigns.
24 January:	Société Générale announces that its trader Jerome Kerviel has 'lost' €4.9 billion, and the bank €2 billion in the sub-prime crisis.
11 February:	The Fed announces that sub-prime losses will not be $50 billion but in fact $400 billion.
14 March:	With Bear Stearns in collapse, the Fed rescues it through JPMorgan getting a loan of $30 billion and a guarantee to secure Bear Stearns.
2 April:	Lehman Brothers announces a capital gain of $4 million.
9 June:	Lehman Brothers announces a second quarter loss of $2.8 billion. President Richard Fuld asks his Director General, Joe Gregory, to resign.
1 July:	Bank of America takes over Countrywide Financial for $2.5 billion.
30 July:	President Bush proposes a rescue plan of the housing market, $300 billion.

26 August: The FDIC (Federal Deposit Insurance Corporation), guarantor of the accounts in 8,600 American banks, reveals a black-list of 117.

31 August: Allianz Insurance sells Dresdner Bank to Commerzbank.

7 September: The Fed guarantees Fannie Mae and Freddie Mac debt at $100 billion each. Effectively this is a nationalisation.

10 September: Lehman Brothers declares a $3.9 billion loss in its third quarter.

14 September: Barclays seems ready to rescue Lehman but then asks for a public guarantee like JPMorgan had with Bear Stearns. The Fed and the Treasury refuse. Lehman is forced to declare bankruptcy.

15 September: The government's refusal to rescue Lehman causes a market upheaval. The E.C.B. releases €100 billion into the market.

16 September: AIG, the American global insurer, is on the edge of collapse. The Fed is forced to bring $85 billion against 79.9% of its capital.

19 September: Henry Paulson, the Treasury Secretary,

proposes a $700 billion package to buy up the banks' toxic debt.

25 September: Washington Mutual collapses. JPMorgan takes it over, making itself the leading U.S. deposit bank.

29 September: The U.S. Congress reject the Paulson plan.

2 October: Wells Fargo takes over Wachovia, America's fourth bank.

3 October: The Paulson plan redesigned as a general rescue is adopted by Congress and backed by Bush.

9 October: Iceland forced to nationalise three banks and beg aid from Russia. Japan's Yamato Life Insurance declares bankruptcy.

24 October: The IMF grants emergency loans to Iceland, Ukraine, Pakistan, Argentina and Hungary.

4 November: Obama elected President.

10 November: Public aid to AIG goes from $85 to $152 billion.

23 November: The Treasury injects $20 billion into Citigroup.

11 December: Bernard Madoff, former President of Nasdaq, is arrested for losing $65 billion of his investors' funds.

16 December: The Fed holds interest rates to between 0% and 0.25%.

Thus, at the end of the crisis year 2008 the banking system was forced to withdraw the interest on all its deals, the greater amount of which are exposed as sheer gambling.

In the Spring of 2009 the C.E.O.s of thirteen of America's leading banks met with the U.S. President. They were:

Ken Chenault   - American Express
Ken Lewis   - Bank of America
Robert Kelly   - Bank of New York Mellon
Vikram Pandit   - Citigroup
John Koskinen   - Freddie Mac
Lloyd Blankfein - Goldman Sachs
Jamie Dimon   - JPMorgan Chase
John Mack   - Morgan Stanley
Rick Waddell   - Northern Trust
James Rohr   - PNC
Ronald Logue   - State Street
Richard Davis   - US Bank
John Stumpf   - Wells Fargo

The important thing to recognise is that these

names would have remained completely hidden and unknown to the masses. It was only the financial collapse of 2008 that forced the oligarchic chiefs into the open. It must also be taken into account that they were responsible for the loss of billions of dollars. Yet how can men lose something that was not there in the first place? It was lost but cannot be found. It never had substantial existence, only numerical traces indicating a possibility of existence, which proved worthless. This dilemma which involves the greater mass of modern men is the deepest and penultimate matter in this affair. It implies that the quotidian social nexus is itself a psychosis.

What manner of man – and note the absence of women – is capable of dragging millions of people into this black hole? Before offering an archetypal model of the banker's psychic make-up it must first be noted that the result of the collapse of 2008 was to reduce the number of mega-banks, massively increase their wealth, and then hit the masses while they still reeled from the shock that they on the response of their elected governments had bailed out the financial system with their own funds intended for health, education and infrastructure. The hit was brilliant. It was no longer to cast the bankers as the guilty party but the masses for their enormous debt to the banks. The magic word was deficit. It was time for the masses to pay up! So while the world's industrialised nations disintegrated under the sweeping budget cuts imposed on them – the bankers, with increased profits, rewarded themselves even more than before. The Greek national economy caved in irretrievably while Italy, Spain, Portugal and indeed the USA plunged into poverty and the abolition of social services.

With the withdrawal of medical care, the absence of homes, the radical dismantling of the universities, and a population deep in unemployment, the future social order would be reduced to crowd control. The police became, uniquely, responsible for the state's stability. In short, civil war had become the norm of the future.

The Roman Catholic Church, faced with a growing rational awareness brought about by the intellectual dynamics of Erasmus, Henry VIII and the slow but irrevocable eroding of superstition by the chivalric orders, found themselves forced to introduce more protective protocols rather than cede to reason's increasing pressure.

In the days of their medieval power the Catholic Church de-regulated Hell with the invention of Purgatory, thus allowing an increased power to the priests to move people up and out of Hell in stages by the payment of indulgences and the hiring of Masses. Faced with the deflation of power after the Renaissance they then passed a series of doctrines insisting on their necessity for mankind. The Doctrine of the Infallibility of the Pope in faith and moral matters. The Doctrine of Bodily Assumption of the Virgin Mary. The Doctrine of Supplication via the Virgin Mary. The Church was moving the faithful away from a sacramental crucifixion faith, now discredited, to a Holy Mother worship.

After 2008 the bankers allowed a heavily shaved Dodd-Frank Act to pass into law in 2010. They then authorised a series of increasingly esoteric doctrines to be part of new banking. 'The Supervisory Capital Assessment Programme' (SCAP): the 'Comprehensive Capital Analysis Review'(CCAR): 'Quantitative Easing' (QE3): 'Large Institution Supervision Co-ordinating Committee'.

What manner of creature is a banker? Speaking in St. Paul's Cathedral, of all places, Goldman Sachs executive Brian Griffiths declared: 'The injunction of Jesus to love others as ourselves is a recognition of self-interest! We have to tolerate the inequality as a way of achieving greater prosperity and opportunity for all.' Goldman's Blankfein insists he is 'doing God's work!'

In 1896, Ibsen presented to the world his vision of the capitalist banker, his penultimate play, 'John Gabriel Borkman'. This, one of the great masterpieces of the Norwegian playwright, tells the story of an investment banker involved in the crash of his bank and forced to spend eight years in prison. On emerging from prison he spends another eight years locked upstairs in his house, seeing no-one, pacing compulsively like a caged animal. The drama unfolds when Borkman comes downstairs to face the intense conflict he has generated in his wife and her sister, who had been in love with him, and his son, fought over by his mother and his aunt. The son breaks free of them and Borkman, his life and his soul laid bare by the unloved family trapped around him, sets out to face the icy mountain above their house only to slump dead of a heart attack. Ibsen portrays the banker as a man whose life was engrossed in the mechanism of acquired wealth, with the illusion that everything happens through his release of the money he controls. At the same time the price that had to be paid was that he lived incapable of love.

Borkman despises the common people. He says:

> 'That is the curse, the burden we chosen men have to bear. The masses, the mediocre millions – they do not understand us.'

He talks of:

> 'The day I am rehabilitated – when they realise they cannot do without me – when they come up to me in this room and get down on their knees and implore me to take over control of the bank again. (He steps by his desk and strikes his chest) I shall stand HERE to receive them. And throughout the land men will ask and learn what conditions John Gabriel Borkman lays down.'

Broken, he still boasts:

> 'I could have created millions! Think of all the mines I could have brought under my control, the shafts I could have sunk.

I would have harnessed cataracts – hewn quarries. My ships would have covered the world, linking continent to continent. All this I would have created alone.'

In despair, he looks back:

'I was so close to my goal. I only needed eight days to consolidate my position. Every deposit would have been redeemed. All the money I had used so boldly would have been back in its place. All the stupendous enterprises I had planned were within a hair's breadth of being realised. No-one would have lost a penny.'

He finally tells Ella, the woman he had loved, his wife's sister:

'As I walked there alone, wrestling with all the great projects I intended to launch, I felt – almost like an aeronaut. Walking the sleepless nights – filling, as it were, some giant balloon in which I was about to sail across an uncharted and perilous ocean... I wanted all the sources of power in this country to serve me. The earth, the mountains, the forests, the sea. So that I might create a kingdom for myself, and prosperity for thousands and thousands of others.'

At the end of that final scene, almost unbearable in its intensity, Ella confirms to him that he had killed their love, tells him that he will never ride triumphant into his cold kingdom. The two sisters join hands at last over his corpse:

'We two shadows – over this dead man.'

So it is not only the whole world which is ruined by the usury of banking, it is also the ruin of the bankers. It is a doomed profession.

VII

Syme writes:

> 'Pedestrian critics in antiquity asserted that Lucan was not a poet but an historian. A juster appreciation of both poetry and history will vindicate his right to the double title – and reveal his kinship with Cornelius Tacitus. ... Lucan and Tacitus acknowledge a similar subject and like preoccupations.'

> (Tacitus, Vol. I. p. 142)

'Lucan's 'Pharsalia' recorded the doom of

republican libertas. Tacitus (was) in a sense
his successor. ...'

(The Roman Revolution, p. 507)

Lucan's 'Bellum Civile', the Civil War or as classicists liked to call it, 'Pharsalia', that battle being
its central subject, was held in the highest esteem
alongside Virgil and Homer. Lucan's headlong
attack on the epic tradition does not diminish his
own majestic position. On the fiftieth anniversary
of his birth, Statius honoured him in an ode presented to Polla, Lucan's widow.

Chaucer in his 'Troilus and Criseyde' wrote of 'The
grete poet, daun Lucan':

'And kis the steppes, where as thou seest pace
Virgil, Ovide, (h)Omer, Lucan, and Stace.'

(Chaucer: Troilus and
Criseyde: V. 1791-2)

Dante praised him in his Divine Comedy, where
he wittily placed Cato, so devastatingly deconstructed by Lucan, as guardian of Purgatory. What
more fitting for a devout Stoic than to be placed in

charge of a zone of heaven invented by the medieval Roman Church?

The sublime Marlowe translated the First Book of 'The Civil War', still preferred again and again over later versions. Admired by Corneille and Goethe, he was loved by Shelley, champion of liberty, who said of his epic, 'a poem as it appears to me of wonderful genius, and transcending Virgil.'

Lord Byron quotes Lucan, saying of himself that he is like Caesar:

'Nil actum credens, cum quid superesset agendum.'

(II. 657)

'Thought nothing done while anything remained to do.'

So, either he had Lucan at hand when he wrote, or he knew it by heart, both of which indicated Lucan as part of his literary landscape. He wrote his cousin, R. C. Dallas, of his 'schoolboy erudition', but only after calling an Ode of Horace 'the most difficult poem in the language.'

A century later and the idea of a writer with a classical background was gone, or reduced to the ignorant scribblings of Robert Graves. At last, at the end of the twentieth century, classical scholarship seemed to awaken to Lucan's epic. As the classicists buckled down to a world of Latin grammar and rhetorical rules, to parallelism, antithesis, anaphora and suasoria, it was not surprising that they lost touch with the world of Lucan – up close – the dismal descent into madness of Nero's last years.

To keep a cool head it is always safest to turn to Mommsen. On Nero, he observed:

> 'As the last of the Claudians, he regarded himself as having the right to annihilate the entire globe – a bizarre mutation of the principle of legitimacy.'
>
> (p. 176)

On Seneca:

> 'Seneca was no strong character but Rome was never better ruled than it was under him. Trajan recognized this. The first five years of Nero's reign were the golden age of Rome.'

'The situation did not change until 62. Generally speaking, the first eight years of Nero's reign were marked by judicious and wise government. ... The death of Burrus (Prefect of the Pretorian Guard) brought a total reshuffle in its wake. Seneca immediately relinquished his position and retired to private life; he had been sustained by Burrus.'

(p. 177)

On Piso's conspiracy:

'This was a genuine attempt to eliminate Nero. Gaius Piso was popular among his peers, wealthy, noble and ambitious. The conspiracy was widespread, largely in senatorial circles, had been planned for years with an incredible degree of ineptitude.'

(p. 178)

(A History of Rome
under the Emperors:
Mommsen: Routledge)

According to Suetonius, right at the heart of the conspiracy was Lucan. Scholars have invented the legend that the poet's motivation was literary jealousy, projecting onto Lucan their own emotional range.

To approach Lucan there must first be an outline sense of the soil in which the poem germinated. It was in a closed circle of provincial gentry, not of the old families, but equestrian, of the new cultured elite. Seneca and his family were from Cordoba. Seneca, while Nero's tutor and guide, virtually ruled the Empire in the early days of promise mentioned by Mommsen. His nephew, Lucan, was favoured and granted the role of quaestor before the legal age required. His uncle was Gaius Galerius, Prefect of Egypt. His brother, Lucius Annaeus Mela, was Lucan's father. Thus in the Senecan circle one is dealing with the very core of Empire. Both Seneca and Mela were enormously rich. Tacitus speaks of Nero's 'ravenous desire' for Mela's fortune and it provided motive enough for the Emperor to command his suicide under pretext of the conspiracy that had already killed his son. Lucan's mother Aciliya and his wife Polla further extended the influence and network of this remarkable family.

On Seneca's retirement from office his parting with Nero is recorded in detail by Tacitus, and the response of the Emperor.

'His adicit complexum et oscula, factus natura et consuetudine exercitus velare odium fallacibus blanditiis. Seneca, qui finis omnium cum dominante sermonum, grates agit; sed instituta prioris potentiae commutat, prohibet coetus salutantium, vitat comitantes, rarus per urbem, quasi val-etudine infensa aut sapientiae studiis domi attineretur.'

(Annals XIV. 56)

'To these words the emperor added embraces and kisses; for he was formed by nature and trained by habit to veil his hatred under delusive flattery. Seneca thanked him, the usual end of an interview with a despot. But he entirely altered the practices of his former greatness; he kept the crowds of his visitors at a distance, avoided trains of followers, seldom appeared in Rome, as though weak health or philosophical stud-ies detained him at home.'

The departure of Seneca from Rome and the Emperor marks the point at which, all intellectual restraint removed, Nero's descent into madness is unleashed. Within the shortest time the assassinations and commands to suicide began. It would end only with the elimination of Nero and most of his enemies. It would effectively wipe out the Senecan family.

At the heart of the conspiracy organised by Calpurnius Piso lie the surviving intellectuals who, in opposing Nero, are well aware of the sophisticated illusion called the Augustan Principate and the fatal error of dynastic rule slavishly unchecked permitting the dismal parade of Julio-Claudian D.N.A., Tiberius, Caligula, Claudius and finally, Nero.

Not only the vanishing old aristocracy but also the new and cultured equestrian and provincial class knew their past. They were acutely aware of the drift from old republican values and they had just lived the post-Tiberian nightmare of an Empire with a paralysed and obedient Senate. They were living, in modern terms, in what should be called a constitutional democracy. In short, the will of the people ignored, and the government slavishly obeying the commands of oligarchic power.

This was an elite which, at least at the dinner table, held to Livy's view of freedom.

Icilius began his argument against Appius Claudius:

> 'Non, si tribunicium auxilium et provoca-
> tionem plebi Romanae, duas arces libertatis
> tuendae.'

> (Livy: Ab urbe condita III. 45. 8)

> 'No, if you have stripped away from the
> Roman people the two pillars of our liberty –
> the aid of the tribunes and the right of appeal.'

Lucan lives and declares the post-Livian values.

> 'Pereunt discrimine nullo
> amissae leges et, pars vilissima rerum,
> certamen movistis, opes.'

> (Lucan III. 119)

> 'The laws are lost and perish

with no crisis, but you, wealth,
the lowest part of life,
you provoked a fight.'

(Braund p. 44)

Lucan's 'Bellum Civile' is an epic, and today it is
seen as an anti-Virgilian epic, yet it is epic none-
theless, echoing both Homer's Iliad and Virgil's
Aeneid, and he is well aware that he erects his
monument alongside the great ruined worlds of
the past.

Lucan is not the aloof observer celebrating the birth
of a great city which arrived at apparent Augustan
serenity, like Virgil. His epic from its beginning is
to record the ruin of Rome, and thus, the world.
Its opening fires the first post-Virgilian salvo. The
Aeneid opens with Beethovenian certainty –

'Arma virumque cano.' –
'Arms and the man I sing!'

Lucan begins:

'Bella per Emathios plus quam civilia
campos

Iusque datum sceleri canimus,
populumque potentem
In sua victrici conversum viscera dextra
Cognatasque acies, et rupto foedere regni
Certatum totis concussi viribus orbis
In commune nefas, infestisque obvia signis
Signa, pares aquilas et pila minantia pilis.'

(I. 1-7)

Badali's Italian opens:

'Cantiamo guerre più atroci di quelle civili,'

Braund has:

'Of wars across Emathian plains,
worse than civil wars,
and of legality conferred on crime we sing,
and of a mighty people
attacking its own guts
with victorious sword-hand,
of kin facing kin, and,
once the pact of tyranny was broken,
of conflict waged with all the forces
of the shaken world
for universal guilt, and of standards ranged

129

in enmity against standards,
of eagles matched and javelins
threatening javelins.'

(Lucan's Civil War,
p. 3: Braund: Oxford)

War is in the plural, and Emathia means Pharsalus, the great place of confrontation that marked the inescapable endgame of freedom.

Writing on the theme of the Proem of the Bellum Civile the Italian scholar Gian Biaglio Conte says:

'And, for Lucan's ideological and artistic formation, the influence of that great man his uncle was certainly decisive.'

('Lucan': Oxford)

This underlines the political reality that brought about the end of the Neronian dictatorship – a retired chief of staff who knew everything, a young genius of a poet who saw through everything and an epic poem in the making which would tell everything.

In the Bellum Civile the story of the end of Rome, dramatically speaking, begins with Caesar's crossing of the Rubicon.

'Caesar, ut adversam superato gurgite ripam
Attigit, Hesperiae vetitis et constitit arvis,
"Hic," ait, "hic pacem temerataque iura
                                      relinquo;
Te, Fortuna, sequor. Procul hinc iam
                                      foedera sunto;
credidimus satis his, utendum est
                                      iudice bello.""

                                      (I. 223)

'When Caesar crossed the flood
and reached the opposite bank,
on Hesperia's forbidden fields
he took his stand and said:
"Here I abandon peace
and desecrated law;
Fortune, it is you I follow.
Farewell to treaties from now on;
I have relied on them for long enough:
now war must be our referee.""

                                      (Braund: Oxford: p. 9)

Lucan correctly shows that in breaking the law, that is, defying the Senate, he does so in the conviction that the law has already been cast aside, and therefore that the time has come for a new dispensation. The poet underlines that point at which personal character, we would say psychology, impinges on the historical process.

'Non tam portas intrare patentes
quam fregisse iuvat.'

(II. 443)

'He would rather smash the city-gates
than enter them wide open.'

(Braund: Oxford: p. 33)

The last restraining force opposing Caesar, and, ironically, licensed by the Senate, is the military commander, Pompeius. In the same way the Prefect of the Pretorian Guard, Sejanus, represented for Tacitus the last remaining constraint on Tiberius, so for Lucan only Pompeius stands between Caesar and world domination. After the Rubicon we are presented with a man hurtling to his fulfilment.

'Non si tumido me gurgite Ganges
Summoveat, stabit iam flumine Caesar
                                    in ullo
Post Rubiconis aquas.'

(II. 496)

'After crossing the Rubicon, never again
will Caesar be stopped by any stream, not
even if the Ganges blocked his way with its
swollen flood.'

It is this inexorable rushing and hurtling to end-game
which is the music orchestrated with such genius
by Lucan. It is that same urgency and precipitation
which Carlyle recognised in the events of the French
Revolution. Not the events as such, but the tenor of
events – the klang, as musicians indicate, or the sound
people hear in the air during an earthquake.

Lucan, as narrator, records the great confrontation
of the Civil War, the battle of Pharsalus.

'Ergo utrimque pari procurrunt agmina motu
Irarum; metus hos regni, spes excitat illos.'

(VII. 385)

'Thus the armies rushed forward, each inspired with the same passionate ardour, the one eager to escape a tyranny, the other to gain it.'

'Tunc omne Latinum
Fabula nomen erit.'

(VII. 391)

Badali's Italian version has:

'Allora il nome latino diverrà un mito.'

(Badali: p. 365)

'Then all the Latin name will be a myth.'

Here Lucan sounds his profound chordal theme that surfaces throughout the epic.

The epic holds up for us three titanic figures, iconic of three distinct political positions. Pompeius, the old military commander propping up the ruined senatorial principle. Cato, the philosopher idealist made powerful by not entering the struggle. Caesar, the man of destiny, or inner compulsion, who must play out his energy-charge to its end.

Lucan unlocks the frozen perfection of Cato, the
supreme stoic above the storm by confronting him
with Brutus who supports Pompeius and by extension, Rome. Brutus challenges Cato's decision to
side with Pompeius.

'Nimium placet ipse Catoni
Si bellum civile placet. Pars magna senatus
Et duce privato gesturus proelia consul
Sollicitant proceresque alii;
                quibus adde Catonem
Sub iuga Pompei, toto iam liber in orbe
Solus Caesar erit.'

(II. 276)

'If Cato accepts civil war, he accepts Caesar
also more than enough. When half the
Senate, when the consuls and other nobles,
mean to wage war under a leader who holds
no office (i.e. Pompeius) the temptation is
strong; but, if Cato too submits like these to
Pompeius, Caesar will be the only free man
left on earth.'

Lucan has Brutus continue in an extraordinary declaration which shows that there is a cause of Libertas but it is in the hands of a man. It will not be rescued on the battlefield.

'Quod si pro legibus arma
Ferre iuvat patriis libertatemque tueri,
Nunc neque Pompei Brutum neque
                    Caesaris hostem
Post bellum victoris habes.'

(II. 281)

'If, however, we resolve to bear arms in defence of our country's laws and to maintain freedom, you behold in me one who is not now the enemy of either Caesar or Pompeius, though I shall be the enemy of the conqueror when war is over.'

Thus Lucan clearly places Brutus as the marker on Caesar from Pharsalus to Philippi, two battles he juxtaposes in the course of the epic. The two battles are victories, the first for Caesar and the second for Augustus, the new Caesar.

'Sed par quod semper habemus,

Libertas et Caesar erit:'

(VII. 695)

'It was the never-ending contest between Freedom and Caesar.'

Badali has:

'Sarà invece quella degli avversari di sempre, la Libertà e Cesare.'

(Badali, p. 385)

Always, two adversaries, here is the locked determinism of state power. Military power is assured the victory. In the renowned last word of Malaparte in 'The Skin':

' "E una vergogna vincere la guerra" dissi a voce bassa.'

(La Pelle: Malaparte Opere Scelte p. 1329: Mondadori)

'"It is a shameful thing to win a war," I said in a low voice.'

With Pompeius defeated the burden of resistance falls on Cato. Lucan's recounting of Cato's dilemma is macabre. Cato ends up in the Libyan desert where his soldiers are attacked by a horrific infestation of venomous snakes. It is not the Stoic with his philosophy who comes to the rescue but a local primitive tribe which has mastered the science of antidotes. Exhausted, Cato and his men rest up in Leptis by the sea.

It is important to recognise that what we call Stoicism is very far from what we now consider it, a philosophy and a system. Its Roman versions were already far from Zeno. Rather Stoic thinking was already absorbed, in the way Auden spoke of Freud:

'To us he is no more a person
now but a whole climate of opinion.'

(Auden: Collected Poems: 273)

Certainly, that outlook in the face of the horror of Nero's paranoid slaughter, gave both Lucan and his uncle, Seneca, dignity and nobility at their blood-drenched end, but by then both philosophy and reason had been left well behind.

Before turning to Lucan's most profound vision in the Bellum Civile it is important to touch on modern scholarship in relation to Lucan and indeed the classical age.

While modern classicists have recovered a creative and valuable view of Roman texts after the dismal rejection of them in the post-world-war-two ethos of undefined socialism which saturated all thinking and each university, they have succumbed to a new distortion of perception. American academics seem genuinely to believe that they think and function in a free democracy from which they can coolly survey the troubled past and even the European inheritance.

The excellent Shadi Bartsch, who has important things to say, still has bought into the ideological super-frame of America. It is absolutely relevant to quote Hannah Arendt but it is facile to think that her analysis applies to Nazi Germany and then fail to see that it is even more relevant to the capitalist economies of Europe and America. One cannot trot out the political doctrine of the 'unspeakability' of Auschwitz and the genocide. This is pure deification. No subject has been more spoken about, and rightly so, in our time. This means that the unlawful invasions of Iraq and Afghanistan, too, must be confronted. The million victims. The renditions, the concentration camps of Guantanamo and Bagram Base Prison. The sadistic orgies of torture and deaths in Abu Ghraib Prison in Iraq. The collapse of a military machine, with its only capable General fired by an ignorant civilian President, and the soldier in the field massacring sixteen women and children, without reason, only to have it excused as a psychiatric problem. The one vital relevance of Lucan is that he addresses our world in just the same nihil as was the Nero epoch and its own particular psychotic governance, our modern plunge into slavery and quite mad leadership, hiding behind the political class as Tiberius hid in Capri.

In the year 65 in the month of April, Marcus Annaeus Lucanus, our Lucan, on the discovery of the Piso Conspiracy to overthrow the Emperor, Nero had him condemned to a state-ordered suicide. A year later his father and both his uncles would have been driven to the same state execution.

Tacitus is the recorder:

'Exim Annaei Lucani caedem imperat. is

profluente sanguine ubi frigescere pedes
manusque et paulatim ab extremis cedere
spiritum fervido adhuc et compote men-
tis pectore intellegit, recordatus carmen a
se compositum, quo vulneratum militem
per eius modi mortis imaginem obisse
tradiderat, versus ipsos rettulit, eaque illi
suprema vox fuit.'

(Annals XV. 70)

'Next he (Nero) ordered the destruction of
Marcus Annaeus Lucanus. As the blood
flowed freely from him, and he felt a chill
creeping through his feet and hands, and
the life gradually ebbing from his extremi-
ties, though the heart was still warm and he
retained his mental power, Lucanus recalled
some poetry he had composed in which
he had told the story of a wounded soldier
dying a similar kind of death, and he recited
the very lines. These were his last words.'

Near the end of Book Nine of the Bellum Civile,
Lucan speaks in his own voice:

'O sacer et magnus vatum labor! omnia fato

eripis et populis donas mortalibus aevum.
Invidia sacrae, Caesar, ne tangere famae:
Nam, si quid Latiis fas est promittere
                                    Musis,
Quantum Zmyrnaei durabunt vatis
                                    honores,
Venturi me teque legent; Pharsalia nostra
Vivet, et a nullo tenebris damnabimur aevo.'

(IX. 980)

'How mighty, how sacred is the poet's task!
He snatches all things from destruction
and gives to mortal men immortality. Be
not jealous, Caesar, of those whom fame
has consecrated; for, if it is permissible for
the Latin Muses to promise aught, then as
long as the fame of Smyrna's bard endures
(Homer), posterity shall read my verse and
your deeds; our Pharsalia shall live on, and
no age will ever doom us to oblivion.'

A. E. Houseman noted: 'Our Pharsalia – fought by
you and told by me.'

This leads inexorably to the final matter, to the
gold seam of historic ore.

VIII

It is only with Lucan as base camp that modern men can set out to affront the mountain of the future. The terrible landscape of ruined cities, slaughtered tribes and humiliated nations was his. The great heroes of events, of history itself are fraudulent, Pompeius sadly so, Cato inexcusably so, and Caesar unforgivably so. Men are not guiding the affair. System continues but it has destroyed the world. Can we not recognise the catastrophic reality?

When we were told that scientists had discovered

one isolated tribe in the Amazon that had survived totally untouched and without outside contact, did our hearts not soar? When we were shown the aerial shots of them as they fired their bows and arrows to ward us off, did our hearts not sink?

The world system, which is an abstract mathematical grid dominating all transactions and based on an irrational fantasy of perpetual increase run by a hidden, not secret but well hidden, handful of utterly worthless, amoral gamblers and thieves – a group functioning as high priests of the numeric itself – that system is doubly doomed. It is doomed, mathematically, as system. It is doomed because these Titans, as Jünger called them, are in reality despicable dwarfs.

Have they not poisoned the ocean? Have they not polluted the air? Have they not stripped bare the oxygen giving forests? Have they not taken from the poorest peasant the seed with which he grows his crop but then sold him a genetically modified one which a year later will be barren, forcing him to buy seeds from his new masters? Man is no longer enslaved by sword and gun but by the seed which should grant him independence.

Lucan's epic surveys a world not only in ruins but one where all previous values, not high moral values, but the basic rules that once governed war, occupation and terms, have been swept away.

Here, Afranius surrenders to Caesar:

'Campis prostrata iacere
Agmina nostra putes; nec einem felicibus
                                        armis
Misceri damnata decet, partemque triumphi
Captos ferre tui; turba haec sua fata peregit.
Hoc petimus, victos ne tecum vincere cogas.'

(IV. 358)

'Think of our men as lying on
            the field defeated,
For it is not right to mix defeated
            with conquering enemies,
Or for prisoners to share in your triumph.
My army has completed its destiny.
This we ask – that you will not force
The conquered to conquer along with you.'

Yet here men are in our time being first defeated and then degraded by being forced into the service of the occupying army. In Iraq the banking oligarchs, under their military umbrella of a force commanded by U.S. politicians, having bombed the cities for 'shock and awe', then compelled the defeated to 'work with' the occupying force under the pretext of a future freedom once they had become a surrogate police force over their own people. What can be seen in these verses is that when the occupying force leaves, the country must as a result fall into a civil war. This disastrous policy has also been applied in Afghanistan.

Part of the new horror of our time is that today men, that is rulers and soldiers, do not even know how to win a war, as if when gained, they were constricted and ashamed. The Israeli conquest of Palestine dribbled into self-justifying rhetoric, producing a history of ruthless cruelty called peace-keeping and a disastrous rebellion by the conquered based on the old Wilsonian fantasy about 'the right of self-determination', a policy in turn leading to more killing of innocents.

Equally, the Palestinians did not have that sense of honour which permits you to admit defeat. Rotundly conquered, they clung to an ideology of 'rights' and condemned a generation of their own people to victim status in the new peace called terrorism. One of the ugly side-effects of this was that, influenced by the Lebanese, they adopted the Shi'a-Isma'ili practice of suicide-attack. Suicide bombing is itself civil war, for the shamed father drives his own son to blow himself up because he failed as a fighter to win or get blown up. This is the pure Lucanian result of pointless military activity. Degraded by an unadmitted defeat, in the shortest time these miserable people turned on each other in civil war dividing their tiny country in two. Their leaders met together at the sacred Ka'ba in Makkah and swore peace, yet days later they broke their worthless promises and fought again.

For Lucan, civil war is the final political abyss of men. If the United States of America began with at least a pretension to republic it soon took a predictable path, from Constitution and Senate it soon gained great wealth. The path to Empire was swift but it was preceded by a bitter continent-wide civil war. Faulkner, one of America's profounder writers, insisted that the American civic project could never work, built as it was on an indigenous community enslaved in Reservations and a community transformed from the slavery of possession to the slavery of poverty. Thus the history of America from a Lucanian perspective is simple. A people who fought their own people to be free promptly massacred and then enclosed the remnant of the indigenous people in Reservations, that is village-prisons. Burgeoning wealth turned the Americans into a nation divided in civil war. Empire soon followed with the occupation of Hawaii and Puerto Rico and a colonial hand on Panama and Cuba. The great expansion came in the command over Europe's two wars. America blanket-bombed Dresden, Hamburg, Berlin, and nuclear-bombed Hiroshima and Nagasaki. At century's end their forces all but obliterated the ancient city of Baghdad and went on to a decade-long occupation of Afghanistan. Utterly spent in these unproductive imperial adventures, the political system disintegrated, ceding an absolute fiduciary authority to the banking system that had been dramatically evolving in the space left it by the pointless dialectic of east-west security conflicts. By the new century, in its first decade, the banking oligarchy controlled the U.S.A. and had begun its leveraged buy-outs, no longer of corporations, but of nations. By 2012, Greece found itself governed by an un-elected leader, named a technocrat, meaning, of course, the oligarch's man running the take-over. Italy was to follow. It was the last act of the tragedy, or, more exactly, the last sequence of the action movie. The bankers, billionaires. The State, broke.

'Pauperiorque fuit tunc primum Caesare Roma.'

(III. 168)

'And then for the first time Rome was poorer than a Caesar.'

The present, after a therapeutic reading of Lucan, can be recognised as the re-iterated chordal structure of the Roman symphony in a new setting. It is not that history repeats itself. It is not that this time is worse, now that global survival is finally in question. What was shocking to Lucan and is numbing to us is not the frenzied compulsion to kill and lay waste, not the insatiable greed of the wealthy – it is the passive acceptance of the masses before the dementia of leadership. Just at the point when it might be suggested that this is the fault of the masses' elective activity it has only in the immediate past been laid bare that the leaders are not in charge. There is an all-powerful junta of financiers who do effectively govern human affairs and they were appointed by no known franchise.

However, as a result of this departure from the modern frame of masses choosing a political class to tax them and send their sons off to die for the cause of the day – it is necessary to get at the disaster of political democracy before bringing forward the small but terrible few thousand who hold the world to ransom.

Rome presents a dynamic of changing modes of power to deal with its evolution and setbacks. Its first age was of elected kings. King Numa minted coin, outlined Rome's boundaries, established divine worship and claimed revelation from Jupiter.

Under Servius Tullius a census was created, with office based on property ownership. The timocratic State was thus established for the full Republican era. With Tarquin elected kingship ended after 244 years. Lucius Iunius Brutus established the Republic, 509 BC.

The Senate was an unelected body with no constitutional powers but with great influence. From it the Roman electorate chose its magistrates. A new magistracy, the quaestorship, was created to run finances and the treasury. In times of crisis one man became dictator.

121 years into the Republic it was briefly defeated by the Gauls. After this the Republic entered into a phase of almost continual wars. The main phase of the Punic Wars brought Scipio's defeat of Hannibal in 202 BC. The magistracies were now military commands. Territorial expansion defined the economy. In 146 BC Carthage was finally destroyed.

First Republican proposition: a Republic is an instrument of war.

Second Republican proposition: an absence of war makes civil war inevitable.

> 'Ceterum mos partium et factionum ac deinde omnium malarum artium paucis ante annis Romae ortus est otio atque abundantia earum rerum, quae prima mortales ducunt. Nam ante Carthaginem deletam populus et senatus Romanus placide modesteque inter se rem publicam tractabant, neque gloriae neque dominationis certamen inter civis erat; metus hostilis in bonis artibus civitatem retinebat.
>
> Sed ubi illa formido mentibus decessit,

scilicet ea quae res secundae amant, lascivia atque superbia incessere. Ita quod in advorsis rebus optaverant otium postquam adepti sunt, asperius acerbiusque fuit. Namque coepere nobilitas dignitatem, populus libertatem in libidinem vortere, sibi quisque ducere, trahere, rapere. Ita omnia in duas partis abstracta sunt, res publica, quae media fuerat, dilacerata.'

(Sallust: Bellum Iugurthinum: XLI)

'Now the institution of parties and factions, with all their attendant evils, originated at Rome a few years before this as the result of peace and of an abundance of everything that mortals prize most highly. For before the destruction of Carthage the people and senate of Rome together governed the republic peacefully and with moderation. There was no strife among the citizens either for glory or for power; fear of the enemy preserved the good morals of the state. But when the minds of the people were relieved of that dread, wantonness and arrogance naturally arose, vices which are fostered by prosperity. Thus the peace for which they had longed in time of adversity, after they had gained it proved to be more cruel and bitter than adversity itself. For the nobles began to abuse their position and the people their liberty, and every man for himself robbed, pillaged, and plundered. Thus the community was split into two parties, and between these the state was torn to pieces.'

Sallust pinpoints with political clarity the place at which the Republic was marked for disaster. It was an absence of war.

'Ita cum potentia avaritia sine modo modestiaque invadere, polluere et vastare omnia, nihil pensi neque sancti habere, quoad semet ipsa praecipitavit.'

(Sallust: Bellum Iugurthinum: XLI. 9)

'Thus, by the side of power, greed arose, unlimited and unrestrained, violated and devastated everything, respected nothing, and held nothing sacred, until it finally brought about its own downfall.'

So it was that the failure of the Gracchi to set up

small farmers from among the plebs, we would say create a middle class, which, war over, left the rich class getting richer and the plebs sinking in poverty. It was this failed State, the Roman Republic, which could only precipitate into first dictatorship and finally, civil war.

What blinds modern people from recognising their situation in this Roman tragedy is the blinding effect of the universal franchise. The macabre idea that illiterate and today media-controlled masses could choose both the instruments of government and its leaders remains the barrier to freedom. Masses electing government was never a Republican practice. It was projected onto the anarchic and unplanned condition of the French Revolution and established via the Napoleonic cannon-fodder censuses he imposed. Applied to millions in the case of the significant nation, the concept beggars analysis. The term Republic is kept in the rhetoric but the term 'democracy' implies the triumphant political application of Greek freedom, demos meaning the people, although they were a city holding a slave population. No one cares. No one today, probably, even knows. Indian democracy. American democracy. Chinese democracy. Meaning is not permitted in political discourse.

Democracy has become the pre-arranged structure of a demographic unit, mathematically calculated, by definition a two (or more) party State, thus containing, in Mommsen's definition, 'a built-in opposition to pre-empt revolutionary tendencies.' Modern government, using Roman terminology and structures, and housed in copies of Roman architecture, lays claim to something that is its abhorred opposite, oriental tyranny. The modern State pre-designed to fall into civil war and ruin.

Lucan, confronted with the full horror of Rome's only possible conclusion, takes up his astonishing position.

'Hic furor, hic rabies, hic sunt tua
                crimena, Caesar.
Hanc fuge, mens, partem belli
                tenebrisque relinque
Nullaque tantorum discat me
                vate malorum,
Quam multum bellis liceat civilibus, aetas.
A potius pereant lacrimae pereantque querellae:
Quidquid in hac acie gessisti, Roma, tacebo.'

(Lucan: VII: 551)

'Here the rage, here the insanity and here are your crimes, Caesar! Leave in the darkness of shadows, oh intellect, and let no age learn from my words the horrors of civil war. Rather, let our tears be unseen, let my complaint be unheard. Of whatever you did in this battle, Rome, I remain silent.'

Lucan, the epic poet, inheritor of Homer and Virgil, at the heart of the matter, declares silence. In the inverted language of rhetoric, the moment of truth, the true word has arrived.

IX

Thucydides, at the opening of his history of the Peloponnesian War, tells us:

> 'I shall be content if it is judged useful by those who will want to have a clear understanding of what happened – and, such is the human condition, will happen again at some time in the same or a similar pattern.'

In Book Three, writing of Year 5, Summer of 427 BC, he recorded, here in the magisterial translation of our greatest Greek scholar, Martin Hammond:

'And indeed civil war did inflict great suffering on the cities of Greece. It happened then and will forever continue to happen, as long as human nature remains the same, with more or less severity and taking different forms as dictated by each new permutation of circumstances.'

Thucydides is very precise in identifying the direct result of civil war.

'They reversed the usual evaluative force of words to suit their own assessment of actions.'

He goes on to list many examples where moral evaluations or actions are re-defined and viewed as their opposite.

'The cause of all this was the pursuit of power driven by greed and ambition, leading in turn to the passions of the party rivalries thus established. The dominant men on each side in the various cities employed fine-sounding terms, claiming espousal either of democratic rights for all or of a conservative aristocracy, but the public whose interests they professed to serve were in fact their ultimate prize.'

> (Thucydides: Peloponnesian War: Martin Hammond: Oxford World's Classics)

Tacitus gives to the Caledonian leader, Calgacus, his renowned condemnation of Rome.

'Soli omnium opes atque inopiam pari adfectu concupiscunt. Auferre trucidare rapere falsis nominibus imperium, atque ubi solitudinem faciunt pacem appellant.'

> (Tacitus: Agricola: 30)

'Alone among men they covet with equal eagerness poverty and riches. To robbery, slaughter, plunder, they give the lying name of empire; they make a wilderness and call it peace.'

In Book Four of the History:

'Ceterum libertas et speciosa nomina prae-texuntur; nec quisquam alienum servitium et dominationem sibi concupivit ut non eadem ista vocabula usurparet.'

(History IV. 73)

'Liberty, indeed, and the like specious names are their pretexts; but never did any man seek to enslave his fellows and secure dominion for himself, without using the very same words.'

In Book Eleven of the Annals:

'Falso libertatis vocabulum obtendi ab iis qui privatim degeneres, in publicum exitiosi, ninil spei nisi per discordias habeant.'

(Annals XI. 17)

'The name of liberty was a lying pretext in the mouths of men who, base in private, dangerous in public life, had nothing to hope except from civil discord.'

This, the most profound and lowest depth of politics and the cause of the disintegration of the social project, is openly confronted by Sallust:

'Iam pridem equidem nos vera
Vocabula rerum amisimus.'

(Sallust: B. C. LII. 11)

'The truth is we have long since lost
The true names of things.'

The names of things. This means the naming of
things. Naming is the link between the creature
and creation. It is the differentiating faculty. It
indicates thresholds, limits, indications. The name
itself is the primal signal of language. By language
the human social group are able to give both
order and meaning to lived existence. Language,
significantly, in this it is the opposite of species,
begins in great complexity and runs down and dies
by simplifications. It begins capable of sustaining
long memorised folk records passed through generations, but it ends a grammar fragmented creole
that can only point and name.

Sallust's complaint is against that damaging of com-
munication that is the result of deliberate destruction. He is referring to the falsification of names and
thus evaluations brought on by the moral collapse of
men desirous of power and wealth and status.

In the Lucanian vision words have become their opposite and man stands at the brink of silence – that is to say – the human social project has failed. Incommunicado. In other words, or in another word – madness.

This breakdown resulting in the denial of true meaning to words is the result, is the effect of civil war. In our day rioting in the streets in great numbers IS civil war. Father fights son. Terrorism, its side-effect, father gets son to blow himself up.

The passivity of today's masses results from the helplessness of a life in which a non-existent money system has seen them born into debt, life enslaved by it, and future never free of it. It is not even metaphysical, having no physicality to transcend. It is number but abstract, cumulative, totalising. It is not a thing. It has, if sanity is to return, no name.

A particularly obnoxious English writer had a book entitled 'The Invention of Scotland' proposing it was created as a fantasy of eighteenth century England. Significantly he authenticated the Hitler Diaries which then proved a forgery. The reality of Scotland is a very different matter and it is not a product of imagination. There is a most important book which authenticates the Scottish presence in the world: 'Scottish Hill and Mountain Names' by Peter Drummond. In it we learn that every hill, every mountain, every significant rock in the Scottish Highlands has a name. These names are in four languages, two, Brittonic Welsh and Old Norse, are dead, one, Scots, lingers on beside English, and Gaelic now spoken by a small number of people in the Western Isles and Highlands.

The word 'sgùrr' is defined in Dwelly's Gaelic Dictionary as a high sharp-pointed hill. The contemporary Gaelic poet, Sorley MacLean, wrote of one such crag in the Cuillins of Skye:

'Ach Sgùrra nan Gillean sgùrr as fheàrr dhiubb,
An sgùrra gorm-dhubh craosach laidir,
An sgùrra gallanach cadl cràcach,
An sgùrra iargalta mor gàbhaidh,
An sgùrra Sgitheanach thar chàich dhiubh.'

'Sgùrr nan Gillean the best sgùrr of them,
The blue-blacked gape-mouthed strong sgùrr,
The sapling slender horned sgùrr,
The forbidding great sgùrr of danger,
The sgùrr of Skye above the rest of them.'

After the Jacobite uprising to restore a Stuart kingdom the English punished the Highlands. Children who insisted on speaking Gaelic had boiled pebbles forced into their mouths. The first Census taken re-created all the towns, villages, and topography with new names or phonetic alterations to the old names, Glasgow and Inverness invented, newly coined. Hotels were set up to replace Highland hospitality, now banned as subversive.

Visiting a Highland estate I thought of buying, the present author walked the hills with the guardian. On a rocky ledge stood a large ram. The English when they cleared the Highlands of clansmen, re-settling them by slave ships to Nova Scotia and Tasmania, covered the empty hills with sheep. I turned to the Gillie and said, 'Of course, I'd get rid of these sheep. I'd put cattle here.' The man was clearly moved, almost in tears. He looked long at me then said, 'That rock – in Gaelic – is called the Rock of the Bull!'

Losing language is losing reality. Clear language is sanity itself.

The great German poet, Rainer Maria Rilke wrote:

'Bringt doch der Wanderer
    auch vom Hange des Bergrands
nicht eine Hand voll Erde ins Tal,
    die Allen unsägliche, sondern
ein erworbenes Wort, reines,
    den gelben und blaun
Enzian. Sind wir vielleicht hier,
    um zu sagen: Haus,
Brücke, Brunnen, Tor, Krug,
    Obstbaum, Fenster, –
höchstens: Säule, Turm . . . .
    aber zu sagen, verstehs,
oh zu sagen so, wie selber die Dinge niemals
innig meinten zu sein.'

(The Ninth Duino Elegy: Rilke
Trans. Stephen Mitchell
Random House)

For when the traveller returns
    from the mountain-slopes into the valley,
he brings, not a handful of earth,
    unsayable to others, but instead
some word he has gained,
    some pure word, the yellow and blue
gentian. Perhaps we are here
    in order to say: house,

bridge, fountain, gate, pitcher,
    fruit-tree, window—
at most: column, tower . . . .
    But to say them, you must understand,
oh to say them more intensely
    than the Things themselves
ever dreamed of existing.

At the centre of this ruined world is the lack of recognition of the Divine. The age is both atheist and bankrupt. Man has been reduced to being a debtor when the world is rich and full. The atheist is indeed at the core of the disaster, having mistaken the idea of god for Divinity. Rightly he rejects theism. So too, do the Muslims. The reality of man is that he has a dynamic opening to the Divine. Language itself. Man is designed for language. It lies embedded in the tongue, the glottis, the throat and vocal chords. And the speech is the door to wisdom. The declaration of knowledge begins with a phrase containing a necessary negation before confirming the Real.

لَا إِلَٰهَ إِلَّا ٱللَّٰه

'There is no god – except Allah.'

From this follow the obigations of Divine worship. The Divine is Named. It has no thingness. With this situation however, comes the initiation which is naming itself.

Allah the Exalted declares (2: 29-32):

وَإِذْ قَالَ رَبُّكَ لِلْمَلَٰٓئِكَةِ إِنِّي جَاعِلٌ فِى ٱلْأَرْضِ خَلِيفَةً قَالُوٓاْ أَتَجْعَلُ فِيهَا مَن يُفْسِدُ فِيهَا وَيَسْفِكُ ٱلدِّمَآءَ وَنَحْنُ نُسَبِّحُ بِحَمْدِكَ وَنُقَدِّسُ لَكَ قَالَ إِنِّىٓ أَعْلَمُ مَا لَا تَعْلَمُونَ ۝ وَعَلَّمَ ءَادَمَ ٱلْأَسْمَآءَ كُلَّهَا ثُمَّ عَرَضَهُمْ عَلَى ٱلْمَلَٰٓئِكَةِ فَقَالَ أَنۢبِـُٔونِى بِأَسْمَآءِ هَٰٓؤُلَآءِ ان كُنتُمْ صَٰدِقِينَ ۝ قَالُواْ سُبْحَٰنَكَ لَا عِلْمَ لَنَآ إِلَّا مَا عَلَّمْتَنَآ إِنَّكَ أَنتَ ٱلْعَلِيمُ ٱلْحَكِيمُ ۝ قَالَ يَٰٓـَٔادَمُ أَنۢبِئْهُم بِأَسْمَآئِهِمْ فَلَمَّآ أَنۢبَأَهُم بِأَسْمَآئِهِمْ قَالَ أَلَمْ أَقُل لَّكُمْ إِنِّىٓ أَعْلَمُ غَيْبَ ٱلسَّمَٰوَٰتِ وَٱلْأَرْضِ وَأَعْلَمُ مَا تُبْدُونَ وَمَا كُنتُمْ تَكْتُمُونَ ۝

When your Lord said to the angels,
'I am putting a khalif on the earth,'

they said, 'Why put on it one
who will cause corruption on it
and shed blood
when we glorify You with praise
and proclaim Your purity?'
He said, 'I know what you do not know.'

He taught Adam the names of all things.
Then He arrayed them before the angels and said,
'Tell me the names of these
if you are telling the truth.'

They said, 'Glory be to You!
We have no knowledge
except what You have taught us.
You are the All-Knowing, the All-Wise.'

He said, 'Adam, tell them their names.'
When he had told them their names,
He said, 'Did I not tell you that I know
the Unseen of the heavens and the earth,
and I know what you make known
and what you hide?'

(The Noble Qur'an: Meanings:
Abdalhaqq and Aisha Bewley)

The Message was revealed over some years to the last of the Messengers, peace be upon him, from the All-High Creator of the Universe.

مُحَمَّدٌ رَّسُولُ أللَّهِ

'Muhammad is the Messenger of Allah.'

From this follow the rules of trust-based trade and the abolition of usury, even to a blade of grass. The capitalist investment economy is replaced by an exchange economy.

Among the many things he told his Companions, quite apart from receiving Revelation, there are two that connect us to the Lucanian age, so clearly here anew and recognisable by us as this time of collapse.

He, peace be upon him, and Allah's blessing, told us that there would be no time from his time until the end of time that would not be worse than the time before it.

He, peace be upon him, and Allah's blessing, also told us that if the end of the world should come upon you while you were planting a tree – continue to plant the tree.

— FINIS —

POSTFACE – LA GUERRE CIVIL

Les Romains ont déployé en vivant un large éventail, qui va de l'art de jouir à l'art de mourir, avec entre les deux le courage, la gravité, l'infamie et la tristesse. C'est pourquoi leur histoire est un microcosme de toute l'Histoire: si on connaît bien l'histoire romaine, il n'est pas indispensable de connaître l'histoire du monde; tout ce qui est opus romanum est opus humanum, tout ce qui est œuvre romaine est œuvre humaine.

(Henri de Montherlant:
Théâtre: p. 1311: Pléiade)

BIBLIOGRAPHY

TACITUS: I have used the Fisher text for the
             History and the Annals, for Agricola,
             Winterbottom and Ogilvie: Oxford.
             Translation I have taken from the new
             Everyman edition.

LUCAN: For the Roman I have used the Badali
             text (U.T.E.T.) as the best today. Also,
             Shackleton Bailey and Duff. In trans-
             lation Braund is exact but missing fire.
             Book One remains superbly rendered
             by Marlowe. Badali's Italian is under-
             standably sympathetic.

SALLUST: Loeb Library: Rolfe: Harvard

LIVY: History of Rome: Foster: Loeb,
             Harvard

The Noble Qur'an:	trns. Abdalhaqq and Aisha Bewley (Bookwork)

Roche, Marc: La Banque (Albin Michel)
I have used the 2nd Annex of this important book for its chronological research on the fateful 2007-8 collapse of the banking system. The book is the first European recognition that a historical shift has taken place with an oligarchy in crisis.

* * * * *

Auden, W:	Collected Poems (Random House)
Brandeis, L:	Other People's Money (F. A. Stokes)
Byron, Lord:	Letters Vol. 2 (Murray)
Conte, G.B:	Lucan (Oxford)
Didion, Joan:	Political Fictions (Knopf)
Drummond, P:	Scottish Hill and Mountain Names (S.M.T.)
Eliot, T. S.:	Collected Poems (Faber)
Haynes:	The History of Make-Believe (California)
Ibsen, H:	Plays: trans. Meyers (Methuen)
Josephson, M:	The President Makers (Ungar)
Leech:	In the Days of McKinley (A.P.B. Press)

Bibliography

Machiavelli:	Le Prince (PuF)
Malaparte, C:	Opere Scelte (Mondadori)
Mommsen:	A History of Rome under the Emperors (Routledge)
Montherlant:	Théâtre (Pléiade)
Rilke, R.M.:	Duino Elegies: trans. Stephen Mitchell (Random House)
Roosevelt, T:	Letters vol. 1 & 2 (Harvard)
Syme, Ronald:	The Roman Revolution (Oxford) Tacitus vols. 1 & 2 (Oxford) Sallust (California)
Thucydides:	Peloponnesian War: trans. Martin Hammond (Oxford)